GOD'S WORD A.D.

New Testament Highlights

by LeRoy Lawson

You may obtain a 64-page leader's guide to accompany this paperback. Order number 41023 from Standard Publishing or your local supplier.

A Division of Standard Publishing
Cincinnati, Ohio 45231
No. 41022

© 1983 the STANDARD PUBLISHING Co.,
Division of STANDEX INTERNATIONAL Corp.

Library of Congress Cataloging in Publication Data

Lawson, E. LeRoy, 1938-
  God's word A.D.

  1. Bible. N.T.—History of Biblical events.
I. Title.   II. Title: God's word A.D.
BS2407.L38   1983   225.9'5   83-348
ISBN 0-87239-668-1

Printed in U.S.A.   1983

Table of Contents

The New Testament Setting

Luke 2:1-8; Acts 26

The title is misleading. Calling it *The New Testament* makes it sound like one book, which it is and it isn't. Much of the confusion in Bible interpretation can be charged to the leather binding that holds sixty-six separate writings together, thirty-nine of them in what we call the Old Testament and twenty-seven of them in the New. Unless you remind yourself they were authored by various men at different times to specific audiences for separate purposes, you can badly misuse the Bible, even when you think you are being true to the Scriptures.

It is not inappropriate for the books to be bound together as one, however, since it is possible to trace a common theme through the entire Bible. I like the way Gardner Taylor, a famous Brooklyn minister, has stated it: *"God is out to get back what belongs to him."* The Old Testament tells the story of what God did through the patriarchs, the judges, the kings, and the prophets to get His people back to himself. And the New Testament picks the story up with the good news (Gospel) that what God began in earlier days He has now accomplished in His Son, Jesus Christ, who by His death, burial, and resurrection opened the way for anyone who believes in Him to be brought back to God, to whom he belongs. The story ends with God and His reclaimed people living together in happy fellowship (Revelation 21:3, 4).

5

The New Testament Library

The New Testament library of writings is traditionally divided in this way:

Gospels: Matthew, Mark, Luke, and John

Four different authors tell in their own ways what God has done through Jesus to get back what belongs to Him. The Gospels are not really biographies, since they tell very little of Christ's life except the last three years—and they deal quickly with most of this period except the final week, which they examine in more detail. They are Gospels—accounts of the good news of God's mission to rescue the human race through Jesus.

History: Acts of the Apostles

The Gospel author Luke continues his story, beginning with the ascension of Christ to the Father. He writes of the origin and growth of the church, the body of Christ, which continues the work of Jesus in getting back what belongs to God.

Letters

These are more formally called Epistles, a synonym for Letters. There are twenty-one of them, with thirteen carrying the name of Paul as writer (nine of these being addressed to churches and four to individuals). Hebrews is anonymous, but it is frequently ascribed to Paul. Other letters carry the names of James, Jude, and Peter. Three have no names in the original manuscripts, but because they sound so much like the fourth Gospel they have traditionally been called 1, 2, and 3 John.

Prophecy: Revelation

This strange book seems out of place in the New Testament, but it did not surprise first-century Christians. Known as apocalyptic literature, many works similar to Revelation were in circulation then among Jews and Christians. Revelation's basic message is that God will succeed in getting back what belongs to Him!

Though much writing was done in the first century, the twenty-seven books of the New Testament stand apart from the others. Most of these writings were quickly recognized and treasured by early Christians as authoritative accounts of Christ and His growing church. It is now generally agreed that all the New Testament books were written before the end of the first century, some long before the end of it. Probably three of the four Gospels, Acts, and most of Paul's letters were completed by A.D. 65. This was only thirty-five years after Christ's departure. The point of mentioning this is to remind you that when these Scriptures were being read in churches, many who were listening had been eyewitnesses of the events recorded. Had the writings been in error, the witnesses could have challenged them on the spot and the churches would have rejected them. They believed these Scriptures to be true.

By the way, you may be interested to know that there are about four thousand Greek manuscripts of all or part of the New Testament, with the oldest of them (Codex Vaticanus and Codex Sinaiticus) dating back to A.D. 350. That is far, far better manuscript evidence than we have for the works of Homer, Plato, Julius Caesar, Tacitus, or any other ancient author.

A word about the name, *New Testament*. Obviously it indicates that something drastic has happened to replace the Old Testament (or Old Covenant, or Old Agreement) between God and His people. The Old Testament or Old Covenant calls attention to several agreements God made: one when He chose Abraham to father His people, another when He called Moses to lead His people to freedom and to deliver the law to them, yet another when He established the throne of David forever. In the pages of the Old Testament, however, we find the prophet Jeremiah predicting that a new day would dawn when God would draw up another covenant with the house of Israel, when all of His people would really know Him (Jeremiah 31:31-34).

"That day has dawned," the writings of the New Testament announce. Through Jesus Christ, God has written a new agreement with His people. In one way or another, every book of the New Testament touches on what life in the New Covenant is like, what God has done for us in Christ, and what our appropriate response must be.

Before starting our study of the Scriptures themselves, a little history will help us understand something of the New Testament setting.

A New Day Dawning

We have heard these words for so many years we take them for granted: "In those days Caesar Augustus issued a decree that a census should be taken of the entire Roman world" (Luke 2:1). With this sentence Luke plunges us into the drama of Roman history. The Christmas story is not a fairy story for children, like the adventures of Dorothy somewhere over the rainbow. The New Testament depicts real life in the dust and hills along the shores of the Mediterranean Sea. Center stage is Palestine (which took its name from the Philistines who occupied the small southwestern section of it centuries earlier), the natural bridge connecting three continents, Europe, Asia, and Africa. Its primary actors are the two Israels of God.

The first Israel came from Egypt to invade the territory God promised, then spent centuries defending themselves and their land against a succession of challengers like the Egyptians, Assyrians, Babylonians, Persians, Greeks, and finally the Romans. When Israel is spoken of, this nation of descendants of Abraham is usually meant.

But there is another Israel. Paul speaks of the church as the Israel of God (Galatians 6:16). The Old Testament records the history of the nation of blood descendants of Abraham; the New narrates the story of a new Israel, descendants of Abraham by their faith in God through Christ (Romans 4).

Anything but fairy tales, both Testaments tell about God's efforts to save His real people from the dangers of their very real world.

The Caesar Augustus mentioned so casually by Luke is the same Octavius, adopted son of Julius Caesar, who with ruthless brilliance wrested control of the Roman Empire from his rivals Antony and Lepidus. Augustus welded the republic into an empire and presided over its unprecedented peace. It had been a while since Palestine had experienced any peace. Let us pause for a glance at the end of the Old Testament and the years between the Old Testament and the New.

Much of the Old Testament history is the record of Israel's bloody wars. The centuries immediately preceding the New Testament era were as bloody as the rest. First there were the Assyrians who swooped into Palestine and carried off the northern kingdom of Israel (722 B.C.). Then Nebuchadnezzar's Babylonians carried the southern kingdom of Judah into captivity in the sixth century B.C. As things happen with empires, it was soon Babylon's turn to fall when Cyrus the Great led a siege against it in 539-538 B.C. Babylon's tragedy was Israel's hope, however, since Cyrus reversed Babylon's captivity policies. He issued a decree permitting Jewish exiles to return to Palestine to rebuild their homeland. One of Cyrus' successors, Darius, ruled Persia while the prophets Haggai and Zechariah chided the Israelites for dallying in their temple reconstruction project. Under their constant scolding and Darius' indulgence, the temple was rebuilt. It stood until it was rebuilt on a grander scale by Herod.

Ezra the priest returned to his homeland to teach the law to the former exiles, recalling them to a more faithful walk with God. Nehemiah also worked among them, superintending the rebuilding of the city walls. Old Testament history breaks off at this point, with the Jews home again and their temple once more at the center of their lives.

Greece 331-64 B.C.

Between the Testaments the clashes of the nations continued. For a while Greece was in the ascendancy. Philip of Macedon began the Greek conquest of the world, and his brilliant and restless son completed it. This son was Alexander the Great. In a series of decisive victories, he picked off Phoenicia, Palestine, Egypt, Babylonia, and Persia. But on his victorious return from battle, the invincible young man died. Armies could not kill him, but malaria or drunkenness—we aren't sure which—could. His military conquests were incredible, but his permanent accomplishment was to spread Greek culture and language. From his day on through the New Testament period, Greek was the common language of the Mediterranean world, a fact that greatly aided the spread of Christianity.

Greek culture continued to hold captive the nations Alexander conquered, even after his empire fell apart, and even after Rome in its turn overthrew Greece. There was a little period between Greek and Roman rule of Palestine when the Jews successfully fought off foreign control. From the middle of the second century B.C. until Rome's intervention in 63 B.C., in what we now call the Maccabean period, Jews governed Jews.

Rome

Self-rule was too good to last, however. The Maccabean leaders fell to fighting among themselves. When Pompey of Rome came into the land, one party of them helped him capture Jerusalem in 63 B.C. He then established Hyrcanus as high priest, with the support of Antipater. This Antipater was an ambitious politician from Idumea, south of Judea. He was the father of the Herod who was on the throne when Jesus was born. Politically astute, the father and son kept their power in Palestine for a long time. Cleverly they shifted their allegiance to the winning side in the conflict between Pompey and Caesar, then in the conflict between Antony and Octavius. In time Herod was appointed from Rome as king of Judea and Samaria. After some violent skirmishes with opponents, he secured himself on the throne in Jerusalem in 37 B.C. There he ruled until he died just after the birth of Jesus. You know him as the king who ordered the boy infants of Bethlehem killed in order to protect his throne against the baby who was to be "king of the Jews" (Matthew 2:1-18).

From Rome's civil strife Octavius emerged as Caesar Augustus. He ruled as absolute sovereign, although he was careful to seem more responsible to the Roman senate and people than he was. He drove pirates from the seas and made the ocean safe for commerce. He constructed a highway system that united his far-flung nations into one empire. He even managed to introduce a new—and quite temporary—sense of morality among the ruling classes. And most importantly, he established peace.

In the field of government, Rome dominates the pages of the New Testament. The emperor was supreme, though he ruled through his appointees (1 Peter 2:13, 14). When Herod died, his sons inherited portions of his territory. The one who ruled Judea proved to be incompetent. Soon he was replaced by procurators, direct representatives of the emperor. Pontius Pilate was one of these. In Galilee, however, descendants of Herod held sway for a long time. Herod Antipas, son of the first Herod, was the one who ordered John the Baptist's death (Mark 6:17-28). Another Herod had the apostle James beheaded (Acts 12:1, 2). He was a grandson of the first Herod, but not a son of Antipas. Sometimes he is called Herod Agrippa I to distinguish him from other Herods. His son, Agrippa II, was the one who heard Paul's defense that is recorded in Acts 26.

There is more that should be said, but perhaps this brief sketch will be enough to set the stage for the dramatic action of the New Testament. We see the Jews in the land of Israel with some degree of self government, but subject to the rule of Caesar and his representatives. Roman troops in the land were a constant reminder of subjection, and many Jews were resentful.

10

Test Your Knowledge

Cross out the wrong choice:

1. The New Testament is a collection of (thirteen/twenty-seven/twenty-nine) books.

2. The book of Acts is Volume II of which Gospel? (Matthew, Mark, Luke, or John)

3. Paul (wrote/did not write) all the epistles in the New Testament.

4. Revelation (is/is not) the only book of its kind in the New Testament.

5. (Most/all/none) of the New Testament was written in the first century.

6. We (do/do not) find the names of some New Testament personalities in secular history.

7. The Bible mentions (one Israel/two Israels).

8. The temple where Jesus taught (was/was not) the same building that was built by Solomon.

9. Alexander's greatest contribution to the Mediterranean world (was/was not) one of the Jewish rulers of independent Israel.

No Man Was Ever Born Like This Man

John 1:1-18; Matthew 1:18-25; Luke 1, 2

Four authors provide what information we have about the human existence of this remarkable person Jesus. Three of them tell basically the same story in the same way, so we refer to Matthew, Mark, and Luke as *synoptic* gospels. *(Synoptic* means "seen together," having the same point of view.) John, written later, is decidedly different. At the end of this chapter you'll find a brief description of the four Gospels.

Birth and Character of Jesus

Mark, in a hurry to get into the main action of Jesus' ministry, skips over His birth and early life. John, careful to assure his more skeptical readers of the pre-existence of Christ as the Word of God (the *Logos*), also bypasses Jesus' birth. After his eloquent prologue (1:1-14) he presents John the Baptist's testimony that Jesus is the Promised One of God. On that note the Gospel of John begins.

We turn to Matthew and Luke to learn the circumstances of Jesus' birth. Matthew's account takes care to present evidence that Jesus is the long-prophesied Messiah, so we get a generous sprinkling of Old Testament Scripture along with the narrative. Luke's purpose is slightly different. He works to establish the historical accuracy of the stories surrounding Jesus' birth, having

12

"carefully investigated everything from the beginning." His Gospel relies on accounts "handed down to us by those who from the first were eyewitnesses and servants of the word" (1:2). The two authors agree that Jesus is the duly traced descendant of King David and of Abraham, but Luke traces the genealogy all the way back to Adam, "the son of God." Matthew presents Jesus as the rightful heir of the throne of David and of the promises to Abraham, father of the Israelites; Luke presents Jesus as the rightful Savior from God himself.

Matthew's Account

Many beginning Bible readers stumble over the genealogy with which Matthew begins his account. Don't worry too much about those unpronounceable names. Just remember that the author is writing to Jews, who carefully trace their ancestry back to their beginnings to prove their rightful place among the people of God. They could never accept a Messiah whose lineage was in doubt; He must descend from Abraham and David.

Of course, He must also come from God. So Jesus' human lineage is recorded through His adoptive father Joseph, and his divine origin is attributed to the Holy Spirit. The child himself is Immanuel, which means "God with us," and Jesus, which means "The Lord saves." He has come to "save his people from their sins."

The visit of the Magi (wise men, perhaps astrologers) from the East offers further proof that Jesus is the one the Scriptures have foretold. God gave a strange sign in the sky to signal the birth of the King His prophets had promised. Matthew presents even King Herod's outrageous slaughter of the boy babies as a fulfillment of prophecy. The return from Egypt to Nazareth is not merely Joseph's way of escaping danger in Bethlehem, but also the anticipated fulfillment of prophecy: "He will be called a Nazarene."

Luke's Account

Luke provides much more background information than Matthew does. Writing an orderly account for Theophilus (whose name means Lover of God), Luke provides a little family information, beginning with the birth of Jesus' kinsman John the Baptist. John's birth is miraculous, since his mother is past the age of child-bearing. The angel who appears to his father, a saintly priest, reveals the name and character of his son. The experience leaves the old man mute until the birth of John, when his restored voice was lifted in a paean of praise.

Jesus' birth is even more miraculous. John has two human parents; Jesus is born of a woman, but without a human father.

The first chapter concludes with two magnificent songs praising God for these miraculous births. Mary's Magnificat is sung during her visit to Elizabeth. Zechariah's song praises God for the birth of John—and for Zechariah's ability to speak again.

Luke carefully details the historical moment of Jesus' birth. Let there be no doubt that His birth is a matter of historical fact. It happened in a specific geographical place (Bethlehem), at an identifiable time (Augustus' census of the Roman world), to real people ruled by a genuine emperor. The angels' message to the shepherds announces God's good news to humanity:

"Do not be afraid. I bring you good news of great joy that will be for all the people. Today in the town of David a Savior has been born to you; He is Christ the Lord."

As a child of Jewish people, Jesus is duly presented in the temple to fulfill Scriptural requirements. There the prophet Simeon forsees a remarkable career for the infant.

When Jesus is twelve another visit to the temple is equally remarkable. Already He is about His father's business.

The Nature of Jesus' Ministry

Jesus is initiated into His ministry when His kinsman John baptizes Him. When we examine His baptism, His temptation in the wilderness, the content of His preaching, and the call of His disciples, we can quickly grasp the uniqueness of His ministry.

Baptism
Matthew 3:13-17; Mark 1:1-11; Luke 3:21, 22

All along John the Baptist has known that he is just a forerunner for one greater than he. Although he does not want to baptize Jesus, he obeys because Jesus insists. The Lord must be baptized in order to identify himself with sinful humanity, though He has no sin of His own. John plunges the sinless one into the water of repentance just as that one will later submit himself to a criminal's cross even though He is innocent. He must accomplish what

14

His Father has sent Him to do. No wonder the Father is pleased: "This is my Son . . . I am well pleased."

This voice from Heaven at the beginning of Jesus' ministry confirms that God is with him. Before long Jesus will be under attack, not only from Satan but also from the very people Jesus has come to save (see John 1:1-14). They will not accept Him as the Messiah, because He will not meet their expectations. They want a deliverer who will rescue them from Rome and set up a mighty Israelite throne like that of David. But Jesus brings a new agreement (covenant) between God and His people, one that does not establish a military or political nation but a spiritual one. It will not come into being through armed battle, but through suffering and sacrifice on a cross. The Messiah will be the suffering servant Isaiah foresaw (Isaiah 42:1-4). God wants to get His people back, but on His own terms, not theirs.

The Temptation
Matthew 4:1-11; Mark 1:12, 13; Luke 4:1-13
From baptism to temptation, from a sublime moment of praise from God to a tortured period of harassment from the devil. So soon the battle begins! God has sent Jesus to strike the fatal blow against Satan in a battle of which the temptation scene is but a preview. Satan will use everything in his power—magic to provide everything the body wants, popularity gained through spectacular feats of skill, political power with which to rule the world—to tempt Jesus away from the hard, lonely struggle to permanently pin down Satan.

How grateful I am that the Gospel writers depict this scene immediately following Jesus' baptism! Like Jesus, we find our high moments of obedience and partnership with God are often succeeded by fierce struggles with temptation!

Message: Repentance, Kingdom
Matthew 4:12-17; Mark 1:14, 15; Luke 4:14-28
From the beginning Jesus' message has a central theme: "The time has come. The kingdom of God is near. Repent and believe the good news!" (Mark 1:15).

It isn't an original message. John the Baptist has been urging his countrymen to repent of their sins, "for the kingdom of heaven is near" (Matthew 3:1). John has a limited purpose, however. He makes no claim to be the Messiah, but calls himself "the voice of one calling in the desert, 'Make straight the way for the Lord' " (John 1:23). He promises that another one is coming, "the thongs of whose sandals I am not worthy to stoop down and untie" (Mark 1:7).

He is referring to Jesus. And from His baptism by John until His crucifixion, Jesus also preaches. In synagogues, on mountainsides, from the Sea of Galilee, or in the homes of His friends, Jesus conducts a tireless teaching campaign. His theme bears a closer analysis.

"The time has come." For centuries prophets promised a day of the Lord when God would again move among His people to defeat the enemy. Now Jesus says, "God is fulfilling His promises: now He is coming among you."

"Repent." The Jews cannot claim innocence. Throughout their history they have prostituted themselves with false gods. Now that God is moving to deliver on His promises, they must turn away from anything that separates them from God; they must change their minds, their hearts, their behavior by really trusting now in the one true God and His Son. The word *repentance* is a full one. Its common definition is sorrow for sins, but as it is acted out in the pages of the New Testament it implies a returning to God, a returning that affects the mind (belief), the emotions (sorrow and desire to change), the confession of a new commitment, baptism (the physical act of repentance), and through it all a profound trust in God. Jesus is calling for nothing less than a radical about face, a turning toward God.

"Believe the good news." The *good news* that Jesus speaks of has taken on a richer meaning by the time Mark writes his Gospel. Jesus refers to God's ushering in of the kingdom of God. Mark writes with the knowledge that God's activity includes not only Jesus' life, teaching, and miracles, but also His death, burial, and resurrection—through which He finally makes salvation available to those who believe the good news.

"The kingdom of God is near." In Israel's past, God has been the true King of the nation even though He has ruled through kings or prophets or judges. During the captivity years, however, the political kingdom of Israel vanished. The returning Jews hoped for another kingdom one day, although their leaders taught that it would be more a rule of God's righteousness than a rule of political power. They spoke of "that day" when God would defeat evil in this world and establish justice. Jesus does not explain

what He means by the kingdom of God; instead He takes for granted that His hearers share the dream of God's kingdom. Some think in political terms (Israel will be restored as a military power), some in terms of the destruction of the present world order and creation of a new one. Whatever their peculiar interpretation, they all agree that the kingdom of God means God's personal rule. The time has come for God to confront the world—to confront you—with His claim of sovereignty. Time and again Jesus will return to this theme, and time and again He will ask, in one way or another, "What are you going to do about God's rule in *your* life?"

This sounds too formal, however. While never leaving His central theme for long, Jesus often stresses that the King of the kingdom is not some high and remote monarch, but is instead a loving Father-King. In appealing for our trust and obedience, Jesus cradles these terms in a context of love. We do not just give the Father obedience, but we give Him love.

> The most important [commandment] is this: 'Hear, O Israel, the Lord our God, the Lord is one. Love the Lord your God with all your heart and with all your soul and with all your mind and with all your strength.' The second is this: 'Love your neighbor as yourself.' There is no commandment greater than these (Mark 12:29-31).

In His message Jesus stands in the great tradition of the Old Testament prophets who boldly preached, whatever the evidence might seem to the contrary, that God was taking a hand in human events. Jesus' presence on earth and His deeds of power are evidence that His words of kingdom are to be taken seriously. He has come from His Father with the word of the Sovereign. God will be silent no more. He will speak—He is speaking—through this latest and greatest Prophet.

Jesus announces the kingdom as a present reality and as a coming event. It is present in Him, among His followers, and yet it is also coming. To those who believe, the rule of God is a present reality; to the world as a whole, it is a coming event, when God will assert His rule not over just those who voluntarily believe, but over the entire creation. (See Mark 13:24-27; Matthew 24:29-31; Luke 21:25-28). Our God is King of kings and Lord of lords.

17

Jesus Calls His Disciples
Matthew 4:18-22; 9:9-12;
Mark 1:14-20; 2:13-17; 3:13-19;
Luke 5:1-11; 5:27-32; 6:12-16;
John 1:35-51; Matthew 10:1-42

Jesus selects a dozen men from among the many men and women following Him. For these He has special duties. Some have been fishermen; now they will fish for men. All of them will learn from Jesus. Then He will send them out to do His work when He no longer will be on earth in visible form. They are to live as citizens of the kingdom in which God's will is done in all things; they are to preach like Jesus, heal as He heals, cast out demons, and later, when He has gone, they are to lead His church. They will teach others to continue His ministry until He comes again.

The Gospels at a Glance
Matthew
Written primarily for Jews in Palestine sometime between A.D. 50 and 70.

Purposes

To present Jesus as the long-awaited Messiah, the heir to God's promises in His covenants with Abraham and David.

To overcome the resistance of Jews who expected a different kind of Messiah and to prove Jesus to be the true King of Israel in accordance with Old Testament prophecies.

Characteristics

Generous use of Old Testament quotations.

Emphasis on the kingdom of Heaven (mentioned thirty-three times) and its synonym the kingdom of God (mentioned five times); emphasis on terms of royalty—Son of David (nine times), Son of God, and Son of Man.

Jesus' ministry is primarily to the people of Israel, but not exclusively (Matthew 15:22-28).

Mark
Written primarily to Gentile Christians, probably in Rome during the middle of the first century.

18

Purpose

To persuade readers of the authority of Jesus Christ, the Servant Lord.

Characteristics

An action-packed book with swift-moving narrative.

Little of Jesus' teaching included, but many of His actions.

First ten chapters concentrate on His teaching and healing ministry; remaining chapters present the events surrounding His crucifixion.

Luke

Written for Theophilus, a lover of God (or one loved of God), and other Gentile Christians, probably about A.D. 60.

Purposes

To be the first volume of a two-part history of Christ's ministry and the ministry of the early church (Volume II is the Acts of the Apostles).

To establish Theophilus in the Christian faith through this account of Christ's life.

To present Jesus Christ as Savior and as the perfect man—the Son of Adam as well as the Son of God.

Characteristics

Close attention to detail, the kind of care you would expect from a physician-author.

Careful attention to events surrounding the birth of Christ.

Loving descriptions of people, including many not found in the other Gospels (Zacharias, Elizabeth, Simeon, Anna, Zachaeus, Cleopas) and including many women.

Attention to Jesus' prayer life and the ministry of the Holy Spirit, a theme to be carried out more fully in Acts.

John

Written for Christians in the latter first century (A.D. 85-95) who have been influenced by Greek philosophical thought.

Purposes

"That you may believe that Jesus is the Christ, the Son of God" (20:31).

To establish Jesus as the *Logos,* the *Word* of God at a time when the doctrine of the incarnation (God in the flesh) was under attack.

Characteristics

Most of John's material (90%) not found in the other Gospels.

Many of Jesus' great sermons found only in this book.

Less "action," more teaching than in the synoptics.

Contains more of Jesus' claims about himself in the "I am" statements. (See page 22.)

Test Your Knowledge

1. Which three Gospels are called synoptics?
   Matt , Luke, John

2. Which two Gospels tell of the birth of Christ?
   Matt Luke

3. Which Gospel claims to have been written after careful investigation of the facts?
   Luke

4. Which two Gospels include Jesus' genealogy?
   Matt , Luke

5. Which Gospel includes Mary's Magnificant and Zachariah's song? Luke

6. Which Gospel states in its prologue that Jesus was rejected by His own people?
   John 1:11

7. Why was Jesus, the Son of God, baptized? I John
   To identify himself with sinful humanity, though He had no sin.

8. Define these words from Jesus' message:
   Kingdom of heaven
   Repent A returning to God.
   Good news God's ushering in of the kingdom of God

9. What does Jesus call His disciples to do?
   teach others till He comes again.

10. Which Gospel—
    is the most action packed? MARK
    uses Old Testament prophecies most? MATT.
    was written last? John (?)
    gives most attention to Jesus' prayers? Luke

3

No Man Ever Spoke Like This Man

Matthew 4:12-25; 7:24—8:4

Matthew says that when Jesus concluded His famous Sermon on the Mount (chapters 5-7), "the crowds were amazed at his teaching, because he taught as one who had authority, and not as their teachers of the law." More than once the people must have said of His mighty words and works, "We have never seen anything like this!" (Mark 2:12). Those who knew Him well realized that He had had no opportunity for advanced schooling. He was a carpenter, and thought to be the son of a carpenter. Yet His followers did not hesitate to call Him "Rabbi," Respected Teacher. He clashed frequently with religious leaders, who demanded to know the source of His authority (Mark 11:27, 28). Mark reports that they audited His lectures (2:1-12), criticized His disciples (2:18-22), condemned His breaking of the Sabbath (3:1-6), accused Him of being possessed by the devil (3:22-30), rejected Him in His own hometown (6:1-6), plotted His death (11:18) and carried out their plot (14:43—15:20). Through all their attacks, however, they were unable to beat Him in debate or cause Him to doubt that His word was from God.

It is not surprising that the religious leaders tried to silence Jesus. He taught an approach to God that was new to them—not through law or rites or sacrifices, but through loving obedience to a gracious Father. He taught a new approach to neighbors—by

21

defining a neighbor as anyone in need (see Luke 10:29-37). He taught a new morality, one higher than the one seen in their interpretation of the law of Moses. The Sermon on the Mount (Matthew 5—7) finds the basis of ethical behavior in the intent of the heart, not in the letter of any law. Jesus' way is love enacted; it is suffering rather than avenging, being hurt rather than causing hurt, being perfect "as your heavenly Father is perfect" (Matthew 5:48). Its love For God is reflected in love for others—even one's enemies.

The Gospel of John presents Jesus' teaching in long discourses. Several of His sermons are found only in this Gospel: the new birth (3:1-13), the water of life (4:6-29), the defense of His relationship with God (5:16-47), the bread of life (6:22-71), the light of the world (8:12-59), the good shepherd (10:1-30). John also includes Jesus' famous prayer for His disciples (17:1-26). As most New Testament readers know, it is in John's Gospel that we find these famous *I am* statements of Jesus.

I am the bread of life (6:35).
I am the light of the world (8:12; 9:5).
I am the door (10:7).
I am the good shepherd (10:11, 14).
I am the resurrection and the life (11:25).
I am the way and the truth and the life (14:6).
I am the true vine (15:1).

John's Gospel, so beautifully and simply written, is a good introduction to the life of our Lord. But one of the most distinctive elements of Jesus' teaching is missing in John. He does not include any of Jesus' parables. For these we turn to the Synoptic Gospels.

Parables

A parable (from the Greek *parabole,* which means a placing beside in order to compare) is a literary comparison. It is a story or reference to a simple, everyday event that illustrates a spiritual truth. Jesus takes His parables from everywhere: a thief that breaks in at night, servants that are either cruel or crafty or faithful, a noisy neighbor demanding food for his unexpected guest, a grain of corn growing, a widow pestering a judge, a fishnet that catches all kinds of fish, a father who throws a party for a returning son. When Jesus tells one of these stories, He takes it for granted that His hearers are familiar with what He is talking about and capable of making some judgment about it and about themselves. The parables help His hearers to understand that the kingdom of God has to do with everyday things and everyday people like them.

From the parables we learn several things.

What God Is Like

He is like the father of an erring son who cannot contain his joy when his son comes home (Luke 15:11-32).

He is like a sower who spreads his seed, knowing full well that not every portion of the soil will receive it (Matthew 13:1-23).

He is like a landowner whose tenants have been unfaithful to him and who have killed his servants and his son (Matthew 21:33-44).

He is like the father of a bridegroom who invites his friends to the wedding feast but is disappointed when they do not come (Matthew 22:1-14).

He is like a master who expects his servants to use wisely the talents he has given them (Matthew 25:14-30).

He is like a shepherd who leaves ninety-nine sheep safe in the fold to find the lost one (Luke 15:1-7).

There is more, but this is enough to tell us what Jesus taught about the King of the kingdom.

What the Kingdom Is Like

It is like a field of wheat and tares growing together until the harvest; then it is just wheat (Matthew 13:24-30, 36-43).

It is like a grain of mustard seed that is tiny but grows into a large plant (Matthew 13:31, 32).

It is like leaven that causes dough to rise (Matthew 13:33).

It is like a hidden treasure worth more than everything else a person owns (Matthew 13:44).

It is like a pearl of such worth that a person is wise to sell everything to buy it (Matthew 13:45, 46).

It is like a netful of fish that will be separated, the good from the bad (Matthew 13:47-50).

It is like a king's squaring of accounts with his servant, who is forgiven an enormous debt but who in turn refuses to forgive his debtor, thereby losing his own reward (Matthew 18:23-35).

Major Parables of Jesus

PARABLE	Matthew	Mark	Luke
The Bridegroom, Unshrunk Cloth, and Wineskins	9:14-17	2:18-22	5:33-39
The Sower	13:1-23	4:1-20	8:4-15
The Mustard Seed and the Leaven	13:31-33	4:30-32	13:18-21
The Return of the Unclean Spirit	12:43-45		11:24-26
The Two Houses (on the Sand and Rock)	7:24-27		6:47-49
The Two Debtors			7:41-43
The Children in the Marketplace	11:16-19		7:31-35
The Wheat and the Tares	13:24-43		
The Treasure and the Pearl	13:44-46		
The Fish Net	13:47-50		
The Unmerciful Servant	18:23-35		
The Good Householder	20:1-16		
The Pounds			19:11-27
The Two Sons	21:28-32		
The Marriage Feast	22:1-14		
The Wise and Foolish Maidens	25:1-13		
The Talents	25:14-30		
The Final Judgment (Sheep and Goats)	25:31-46		

It is like a great marriage feast to which the king invites whoever will accept his invitation (Matthew 22:1-14).

The kingdom of heaven is for those who are prepared (Matthew 25:1-13), for those who are good stewards of the talents God has given them (Matthew 25:14-30), and for those who take care of the needs of others (Matthew 25:31-46).

What Is the Kingdom's Citizen Like?

Although entrance into the kingdom depends upon Jesus' opening the way for us, He makes it clear in the parables that citizens of the kingdom have God as their model (Matthew 5:48) as they live on this earth. They are alert for the coming of the Lord (Matthew 25:1-13), faithful in their stewardship of everything their Father has given them (Matthew 25:14-30), and willing to sacrifice everything else for the sake of being in the kingdom (Matthew 13:44-46). They are not anxious about anything, but trust God to bring growth in His kingdom as surely as a seed produces an ear and then the full grain in the ear (Mark 4:26-29). They take care of their neighbors as the good Samaritan took care of his (Luke 10:29-37) and do not hesitate to ask God for help so they can help others (Luke 11:5-8). They build their lives on the solid foundation of Jesus' teaching instead of the shifting sands of human opinion (Matthew 7:24-27), remaining humble before God and patient with men (Matthew 18:23-35). In everything, they remember that God loves them as the father loves his prodigal son and that He will rejoice when they give Him cause to throw a party in honor of their return to Him (Luke 15:11-32).

Jesus' Miracles

Miracles is our English word. The Greek New Testament calls them by three names that can be more literally translated as signs, wonders, and mighty works. *Mighty works* is a good term because it implies that Jesus was using His strength to get things done and to meet specific needs.

There is no doubt that Jesus performed supernatural marvels; even His enemies could not deny them (Mark 3:22). His heart went out to the needy. Compassion moved Him to heal the leper (Mark 1:40-42), the blind (Matthew 20:29-34), and many others (Matthew 14:14). With compassion He fed a huge crowd (Matthew 15:32-38), and raised the dead son of a widow in Nain (Luke 7:11-17). However, His miracles are not simply demonstrations of His compassion. They did help people who were much in need of help, but they had another purpose as well.

Signs also is a meaningful name. Nicodemus saw Jesus' miracles as signs that God was with Him (John 3:1, 2). Peter used them as signs that Jesus was approved or accredited by God (Acts 2:22). Jesus himself presented a miracle as proof that He had power to forgive sins, a power said to belong to God only (Mark 2:10-12).

Jesus' mighty works were an integral part of the message and mission God gave Him. He was sent to preach *and* to do mighty works. Early in His ministry He read the Scripture in His hometown synagogue. The passage was Isaiah 61:1, 2:

> The Spirit of the Lord is on me, because he has anointed me to preach good news to the poor. He has sent me to proclaim freedom for the prisoners and recovery of sight for the blind, to release the oppressed, to proclaim the year of the Lord's favor.

When He had finished reading He told His audience, "Today this scripture is fulfilled in your hearing" (Luke 4:16-21). He, Jesus, is the one who will do all these things. Mighty works are part of His job description. They reinforce His message.

Much later, when John the Baptist hears in prison about the mighty works of Jesus, he dispatches two of his disciples to ask whether he is in fact the Christ. Jesus' answer is straightforward:

> Go back and report to John what you hear and see: The blind receive sight, the lame walk, those who have leprosy are cured, the deaf hear, the dead are raised, and the good news is preached to the poor (Matthew 11:4, 5).

Jesus is doing what the Christ (Messiah) is supposed to do. The language in which He answers John's question calls to mind the Messianic prophecy of Isaiah 35:5, 6. Jesus' miracles herald the dawning of the kingdom of God.

Wonders is the third name given to miracles. This one explains itself. The miracles were wonderful. They caused people to wonder, and some of the wondering people could see the deeper meaning of the wonders they saw (John 3:1, 2).

Bible scholars traditionally categorize Jesus' miracles into four types: exorcisms (casting out demons), healings, nature miracles, and raising someone from the dead. Let's look at a few examples of each.

Exorcisms

Mark tells the dramatic story of the healing of a Gerasene demoniac, a man possessed by a host of demons. We may suppose there are at least two thousand demons, for Jesus casts them out of the man into a herd of two thousand swine (Mark 5:1-20). Matthew reveals that there are two demon-possessed men. Mark and Luke tell of only one, perhaps because one is better known or more violent than the other.

Mark and Luke record that Jesus casts a demon out of a young boy after the disciples have failed to do it. Only Jesus can control the demon (Mark 9:14-29; Luke 9:37-42). Matthew tells the same story, adding that the boy's father describes him as epileptic or lunatic; but Matthew also recognizes that a demon causes the trouble (Matthew 17:14-20).

Healings

Jesus heals every illness known (Matthew 4:23). He forgives the sins of a paralyzed man and enables him to take up his pallet and walk (Mark 2:1-12); He touches an untouchable leper and makes him clean again (Matthew 8:1-3). A Roman army officer's servant lies at the point of death, but without even seeing the servant personally Jesus speaks the word that heals him (Matthew 8:5-13). Because of Jesus the blind can see again (Matthew 9:27-31; John 9:1-7), a man with a withered hand can work again (Mark 3:1-5), a woman with an incessant hemorrhaging is liberated from her curse (Mark 5:25-34), and a man unable to make his way into the pool of Bethesda is cured in an instant (John 5:2-9). And the people are amazed at Jesus' power.

Power Over Nature

The exorcisms and healings are marvelous enough, but even more astonishing is Jesus' control of the forces of nature. What should one make of a man who can feed five thousand persons on two fishes and five small barley loaves (John 6:1-13), or four thousand on seven loaves and a few small fish? (Matthew 15:29-39). What frightening power there is in one whose word can still a storm at sea (Mark 4:35-41) or turn water into wine (John 2:1-11), or who can defy the power of gravitation and walk on water! (Mark 6:47-52). These acts not only place Jesus in the company of history's greatest heroes, Moses and Elijah, but show Him to be even greater than they were (Matthew 17:1-8).

28

Raising Others From the Dead

The most astonishing of Jesus' mighty works are His demonstrations of power over death. When He tells Jairus' little daughter, "My child, get up!" she does so (Luke 8:49-56). When He stops the funeral procession of the son of a widow in the town of Nain and orders the young man in the coffin to get up, the people are "all filled with awe." They praise God to see the boy alive again (Luke 7:11-17). The greatest marvel of all, though, is His raising of His friend Lazarus from the grave after he has already been dead four days (John 11:1-44). There is no explanation of these marvels, except the explanation of faith. This Jesus is indeed a man sent from God (John 3:1, 2). But He is not merely a man. He is God, and the divine power that does the mighty works is His own power as well as His Father's.

His miracles are accompanied by no magical rites, no special incantations, and no mighty struggle with unseen powers. He has but to speak a word and His bidding is done. All His mighty works proclaim the same message, as He once told His enemies: "If I drive out demons by the Spirit of God, *then the kingdom of God has come upon you*" (Matthew 12:28).

For further study of Christ's parables, see the author's Cracking the Code. *For Christ's miracles, see the author's* Lord of Possibilities. *Both are published by Standard Publishing Company.*

Glance over the list of miracles below and on the next page. If you find one you've forgotten, now is a good time to look up at least one of the references and refresh your memory.

Then go on to the end of the chapter and record your reactions to the mini-quiz printed there.

Miracles in John's Gospel

Water into wine	2:1-11
Healing nobleman's son	4:46-54
Healing paralyzed man	5:1-15
Feeding 5,000	6:1-14
Walking on water	6:15-21
Healing blind man	9:1-41
Lazarus raised from dead	11:1-44
Catch of fish	21:6-11

Miracles in the Synoptic Gospels

Exorcism

	Matthew	Mark	Luke
Violent demoniacs	8:28-34	5:1-20	8:26-39
Mute demoniac	9:32-34		
Mute and blind demoniac	12:22-28		11:14-20
Convulsive demoniac	17:14-21	9:14-29	9:37-43

Healing

	Matthew	Mark	Luke
Leper	8:1-4	1:40-45	5:12-16
Centurion's servant	8:5-13		7:1-10
Peter's mother-in-law	8:14, 15	1:29-31	4:38, 39
Paralytic	9:1-8	2:1-12	5:17-26
Blind men	9:27-31		
Withered hand	12:9-14	3:1-6	6:6-11
Hemorrhaging woman	9:20-22	5:25-34	8:43-48
Blind men	20:29-34	10:46-52	18:35-43
Crippled woman			13:10-17

Nature

	Matthew	Mark	Luke
Feeding five thousand	14:13-21	6:31-44	9:10-17
Feeding four thousand	15:32-38	8:1-9	
Stilling storm	8:23-27	4:35-41	8:22-25
Walking on water	14:22-33	6:47-52	
Transfiguration	17:1-8	9:2-8	9:28-36

Raising the Dead

	Matthew	Mark	Luke
Jairus' daughter	9:18-26	5:21-43	8:40-56
Widow's son			7:11-17

Test Your Knowledge

1. What does each of the following parables teach about the nature of God?

Matthew 18:23-35 _____

_____

Matthew 25:1-13 _____

_____

Luke 15:11-32 _____

_____

2. What does each of the following parables teach about the coming judgment?

Matthew 25:31-46 _____

_____

Matthew 22:1-14 _____

_____

3. What does each of the following mighty works tell us about Jesus?

Mark 6:47-52 _____

_____

Mark 2:3-12 _____

_____

John 11:1-44 _____

_____

No Man Ever Died and Rose Like This Man

Mark 15 and 16

Jesus' ministry in Galilee was in many ways a stunning success. Everywhere He went He was cheered by crowds of people who heard Him gladly. He often spoke to them of the coming kingdom of God, but they really didn't know what He was talking about. What they knew was that He could do marvelous signs, so they brought their sick and hurting for His healing touch.

Not everybody loved Him. The religious leaders resented His popularity. Every new healing, every infraction of traditional Sabbath rules, every point He scored in His debates with the Pharisees and scribes stiffened their opposition to Him.

He could not keep going much longer. Everything He did—calling His disciples, eating and fellowshipping with outcasts and sinners, healing the sick and exorcising demons—was an acting out of the nature of the kingdom He was preaching about. The religious leaders did not see it that way, however. They could not, they would not, accept Him as the Messiah. To them He was just a troublemaker. He had to go.

On this point they were in agreement, Jesus and His enemies. They plotted against Him, little knowing that death was very much on His mind also. To prepare himself and His disciples, He retreated into new territory before heading south toward Jerusalem. He needed rest from the pushing crowds of Galilee.

His journeys outside of Jewish Palestine took Him into the region of Phoenicia to the northwest (Mark 7:24), into the region to the east of the Jordan River (Mark 7:31), and north again to Caesarea Philippi (Mark 8:27). In those areas He was safe from King Herod Antipas, who had killed John the Baptist and was threatening to kill Jesus (Luke 13:31). Jesus stayed beyond Herod's reach for a while—and away from enthusiastic followers who were pressing Him to lead a revolution and make himself king (John 6:15).

He also needed some privacy in order to concentrate on teaching His intimate disciples. Before long they must stand alone against the world. They would lead His church. There was much He had not yet taught them.

In all these areas He did have some public encounters. In Tyre He met a woman of remarkable faith (Mark 7:24-30); in the Transjordan region crowds still pressed Him. There He fed the four thousand (Mark 8:1-9) and did other mighty works. But His most important moments were private ones with His chosen disciples.

A turning point of His ministry, so momentous that Mark places the event in the heart of his Gospel, was His quiet conversation with the disciples near Caesarea Philippi (Mark 8:27-33).

Jesus had preached primarily to the multitudes; now He would concentrate on His disciples. Before Caesarea Philippi His message was the coming of the kingdom of God; now He would try to prepare His disciples for His impending death. It was not easy for them to see any relation between the Messiah's death and the kingdom of God. How could the *Christ* be killed? "This shall never happen to you!" Peter blurted out in horror at Jesus mention of His fate (Matthew 16:22).

In rapid succession the Synoptic Gospels move from Peter's great confession (Matthew 16:16) to Jesus' transfiguration and exaltation over Moses and Elijah to His tender healing of the stricken boy (Mark 9:2-29), an unforgettable reminder that Jesus came not to be glorified but to serve the sick and the lost.

Not long afterward Jesus went to Jerusalem and plunged boldly into public teaching and controversy. Repeatedly His enemies were foiled in their efforts either to debate with Him or to arrest Him (John 7—10). After some weeks Jesus defused that crisis by going away across the Jordan (John 10:40). There for a few months He continued to teach both the public and His chosen apostles (Luke 13:22—18:30).

Then with resolution Jesus set out for Jerusalem (Luke 18:31-33). Afraid, His disciples nonetheless went along "that we may die with him," as Thomas said (John 11:16). They went not knowing what lay ahead, but certain of trouble. Jesus knew, but felt He had no choice. He had to carry out His mission.

Crossing the Jordan from the east, Jesus stopped in Jericho. There He healed a blind man (Luke 18:35-43) and met Zacchaeus perched up in his now-famous sycamore tree. The little tax collector would never be the same! (Luke 19:1-10).

After pausing in Bethany and sending two of His disciples ahead to secure a colt, Jesus made what has traditionally been called His triumphal entry into Jerusalem (Mark 11:1-11).

His was not a typical Roman triumph, however. It was expected of victorious Roman generals that they would mount a white steed and proudly lead a parade of captives and other spoils of war through the streets of the capital. Instead, Jesus deliberately chose to enter Jerusalem as a peacemaker, not a warrior. His mount was a humble donkey (see Zechariah 9:9) instead of a horse, the symbol of war. He would not be a warrior king but a servant suffering for peace.

Jerusalem was crowded with pilgrims from all over Palestine and the Mediterranean world. They had come for the Jewish Passover, to commemorate God's deliverance of Israel from bondage in Egypt (Exodus 12). The streets rang with the cries of Jesus' disciples and others who were attracted to the quiet man on the little animal.

"Hosanna!"

"Blessed is he who comes in the name of the Lord!"

"Blessed is the coming kingdom of our father David!" (Mark 11:9, 10).

Jesus' remarkable entrance was followed the next day by His equally remarkable attack on moneychangers and hucksters in the temple. He drove them from their business tables so that at least for a little while the building could once again be what God intended, a house of prayer for all nations (Mark 11:15-18). In the new order he was establishing, God's worship would no longer be centered in a temple so easily polluted by the selfish pursuit of money, but in a Son greater than any temple or priests of the temple.

Not that the priests would give up without a fight! They quickly challenged Him, but He shifted deftly from defense to offense.

He told them His parable of the tenants and challenged them to give to God what is God's. Their hostility hardened. They debated the resurrection with Him and sought to trap Him with other points of doctrine (Mark 11:27—12:40). They could not get the best of Him. He won the debates, but inflamed their hatred as well. His end was drawing near.

In His quieter moments with the disciples Jesus spoke seriously of things to come. Mark 13 records some of His warning. Matthew records more of His urging to watch and be prepared for the coming judgment (Matthew 24, 25).

Tension between Jesus and the religious leaders reached the breaking point by Thursday. Jesus now was ready to give His life. He ate His final meal with His disciples (Mark 14:12-31). Judas had already made plans to betray Him (Mark 14:10, 11).

Even as He prepared to die, Jesus was teaching His disciples. He washed their feet, the rabbi breaking every precedent by becoming His students' servant (John 13:1-17). He took bread and wine and served them, the Servant dramatizing His coming sacrifice. He promised to drink with them again in the new kingdom of God, the one being established through His blood of the covenant (Mark 14:22-25).

This is the only recorded time, by the way, that Jesus mentioned His covenant; but His timing was accurate. At the Passover the Jews annually reminded themselves that they were tied to God through His special covenant with them. Further, the prophet Jeremiah had promised that one day God would write a new covenant with them (Jeremiah 31:31-34). It was not really strange, then, that Jesus should speak of His approaching death as a sacrifice in which His blood would be used to make a new agreement between God and His people. Jesus had lived to announce the new kingdom; now He would die to inaugurate it.

The peace of the night was later shattered by the rumble of the Roman soldiers Judas led into Gethsemane to arrest Jesus. The Lord had been agonizing with God over His coming death, praying that if possible He might be spared what was ahead (Mark 14:32-43), yet willing to die if this was the only way to fulfill His Heavenly mission.

Then followed in rapid succession:

Judas' treacherous kiss. Betrayal disguised as affection, cowardice condemning the Christ, the close and trusted friend turning against his friend (Psalm 41:9; John 13:18).

35

Jesus' arrest. The Prince of Peace surrounded by the minions of war, the Lamb led to slaughter.

His rigged trials. Before the Supreme Court of Israel and the Roman governor of Palestine Jesus offers no resistance, but allows himself to be maligned, lied about, spit at, crowned with thorns, robed in mock purple, and unjustly condemned. The Sanhedrin can try Him, but only Pilate can sentence Him to die.

His rejection by the masses. "Barabbas, Barabbas" is their cry. Better that a criminal be set free than that a Savior be spared.

His death sentence and crucifixion. Lost in the tumult of the moment is the significance that later Christian writers will find. As Abraham pleaded with God for the citizens of Sodom and as Moses interceded on behalf of the wayward children of Israel, so Jesus is lifted up on the cross so that those looking on Him in faith can be saved (John 3:12-18).

He did not die unobserved. Watching Him were calloused Roman soldiers who nailed Him up, then gambled for His clothes. Watching Him were the religious leaders who congratulated themselves on having wiped out a dangerous enemy. With them stood the fickle crowd that every public execution draws like vultures to blood. But there were also the faithful women, including His mother, who could not be scared away by soldiers or swords. And over them all was the watchful eye of God, who seemed to have deserted Jesus in His hour of greatest need but who was really just preparing for history's supreme surprise and Jesus' final triumph.

Theologians have long debated the full meaning of Jesus' crucifixion. All their theories add up to one summary statement: Here on the cross was *proof* of the love of the father whom Jesus came to reveal. Here was the *character* of the kingdom that Jesus was inaugurating, a kingdom of love and suffering—and of victory over the evil one. When Jesus died the temple veil, separating the Holy of Holies from all the world, was torn in two (Matthew 27:51). For centuries it had been firmly in place, keeping men away from God. When Jesus died, the barrier between God and man went down with Him. Jesus' death opened our way to God (Romans 5:1, 2).

The story does not end with Jesus' burial. You can kill truth for a moment, but not forever. You can bury goodness and seal the door of its tomb, but it will escape. Hate can deal love a staggering blow, but it cannot prevail against it. You can nail the Son of

36

God to a cross, but you cannot keep Him there. The cross, the tomb, and the deserted burial linens make a mockery of all human princes and priests who think that theirs is the final authority. They boast that they can plant a crown of thorns on the holy brow, but they can't protect the golden crowns on their own. They seal Christ's tomb to defy God's will, but nothing they do can seal themselves out of a grave. The mockers in the end are mocked.

Had Jesus remained in His tomb, there would have been no New Testament and no church. Everything the disciples later preached and wrote, and everything the church believed rested on the foundation of Jesus' resurrection. God vindicated Jesus when He raised Him from the tomb. The good news that Jesus preached at the beginning of His ministry then took on new meaning. In fact, the apostle Paul summarized the gospel as Jesus' death, burial, resurrection, and post-resurrection appearances to more than five hundred witnesses (1 Corinthians 15:1-8).

The resurrection of Jesus can be compared in significance with the exodus of the Israelites from Egypt. Through the exodus God liberated His people from slavery, an event celebrated in the Passover feast every year. Jesus' resurrection liberates God's people from death itself; they are no longer slaves to yesterday's sins or tomorrow's fears. So Christians celebrate His victory over death every Easter—and every Lord's Day. Christianity's pilgrimage since Christ's death and resurrection has not been one constant success story, but as G. K. Chesterton has written, "Christianity has died many times and risen again; for it had a God who knew the way out of the grave." Because of Christ, Christianity can never be buried.

Test Your Knowledge

Instead of a factual quiz, this is a test of your ability to grasp the meaning of Jesus' death and resurrection—the meaning to people with different points of view. (Based on Mark 15, 16).

1. Ask yourself what Jesus' crucifixion means to:
   —the religious leaders
   —His disciples
   —the crowd that shouted "Barabbas"
   —the soldiers
   —Simon of Cyrene

—Jesus himself
—the women who attended Him
—Joseph of Arimathea
—the person taking this quiz

2. Ask yourself what Jesus' resurrection means to
—Mary Magdalene, Mary the mother of James, and Salome
—the young man at the tomb
—the disciples
—the early church
—the person taking this quiz

5

The Lord Acts—in a New Body

Acts

The Acts of the Apostles is a history book, but you must not expect is to be like any other history you have ever read. It is really Part II of the account its author, Dr. Luke, began in his Gospel. In that volume he sought to give an "orderly account" of "the things you have been taught." The Gospel tells the startling story of someone unlike anyone else who ever lived, Jesus the Christ, and of what He did to get back what belongs to God.

In Volume II Luke continues the story. He still focuses on the activities of the living Lord, but now the Lord acts through a new body, the church. Acts narrates the unfolding drama of the birth and growth of this body in Palestine and beyond.

Luke writes very selectively. If you expect a detailed account of all the apostles or of the country by country expansion of the church, you will be disappointed. Of the original apostles, Luke writes mostly about Peter and John, and very little about the latter. After introducing the first deacons (chapter 6), Luke tells us a little about only two of them, Philip and Stephen. He devotes more attention to Paul than to the original apostles. Although Luke deals with the beginnings of the church, he seems quite uninterested in matters that claim much of the church's attention today: organizational structure, responsibilities of the leaders, standards of membership, and so on.

In a real sense, the main character of the book is not even Peter or Paul. Several have suggested that the title should be the Acts of the Holy Spirit, who is named over fifty times here, more than in any other New Testament book. Very early in Acts, Luke introduces the Spirit (see 1:1-5). From the miraculous work of the Spirit on the Day of Pentecost (chapter 2) through the rest of Luke's report, the Spirit leads Jesus' followers in amazing bold adventures of witnessing and evangelism. It is as if Jesus has told them, "I've done my part. My physical ministry is finished. Now it is your turn—and the divine Spirit that empowered me and raised me from the dead will now be yours." The Spirit's power is not political or military, but more like dynamite. In fact, our word *dynamite* comes from the word used in the Greek. "You will receive *dynamite* when the Holy Spirit comes on you" (Acts 1:8). The church will explode into being and be propelled outward from Jerusalem through Judea and Samaria to the ends of the earth. Throughout the book we discover that Spirit acting—miraculously at Pentecost, quietly many other times—to prepare the way for the preaching of the good news and the saving of men and women everywhere.

But the Spirit is not the theme of the account. He is the means by which the theme is accomplished.

The theme is the kingdom of God. "Lord, are you at this time going to restore the kingdom to Israel?" is the question with which Acts really begins. Even after their three-year apprenticeship with Jesus the disciples have not yet fully understood the nature of the kingdom He preached. His kingdom will not be one *restored* to Israel, like the glorious monarchy of King David, but something quite different. Its power will be spiritual power (1:8) and its territories will be all the nations of the earth.

The word *kingdom* appears only a few times in the book:

The risen Lord speaks often to His disciples about the kingdom, who want to know when He will restore it (1:3, 6).

Philip preaches good news of the kingdom of God and the name of Jesus (8:12).

Paul and Barnabas warn the disciples, "We must go through many hardships to enter the kingdom of God" (14:22).

Paul teaches in the synagogue at Ephesus, "arguing persuasively about the kingdom of God" (19:8).

Paul's farewell to Ephesian elders indicates the burden of his preaching: "Now I know that none of you among whom I have

40

gone about preaching the kingdom will ever see me again" (20:25).

From morning until evening Paul preaches in Rome about the kingdom (28:23).

Luke ends his book on this note: "Boldly and without hindrance [Paul] preached the kingdom of God and taught about the Lord Jesus Christ."

The message hasn't changed. Jesus began His ministry and closed it preaching the kingdom. Paul devoted himself to its proclamation. Luke wrote Acts to describe the birth and growth of the earthly expression of God's complete kingly rule, the church. Church does not equal kingdom, because *kingdom* is the more encompassing word for everything over which God rules. But it is obvious that Luke sees the church as a body of believers in the *Lord* Jesus Christ who give no more than second place to any other ruler in order to be totally obedient to the will and rule of God through Christ.

The disciples' question, "Lord, are you at this time going to restore the kingdom *to Israel?*" receives an answer that they have not foreseen. The problem with their question is that they are thinking of a political settlement to the chronic unrest in the Middle East. But Jesus did not descend with Heavenly power in order to settle a dispute in Palestine. He had something far bigger in mind. He would unleash a force greater than this world had ever before witnessed, stronger than earthly kingdoms, stronger than empires, stronger than civilizations. It would represent God's sovereignty in the universe. On earth its expression would be the church. He would do something never done before: He would establish a body that would be without racial, ethnic, or any other kind of border. It would be unlimited by geography, unswayed by kings, unstopped by centuries, and not limited to this globe. God had earlier entrusted His message to a nation, Israel, and that nation had failed Him. He would not do that again. His new people would know no east nor west, no caste nor outcaste, neither slave nor free, neither male nor female.

No, God would not restore David's kingdom, but would institute something far greater, based on the preeminent Christ, who would be its foundation and its head.

Beginning with Pentecost (chapter 2) Luke traces the amazing progress of this amazing kingdom. As he tells his story, he produces a book of firsts:

first miracle of a new age (2:1-4) *Pentecost*
first sermon of a new age (2:14-40) *by Joel*
first conversions (2:41) *about 3200*
first congregation (2:42) *and they were taught by apostles, fellowship Prayers, etc*
first persecution (4:1-4)
first hypocrisy and discipline (5:1-11)
first deacons (6:1-7)
first recorded sermon by a "layman" (7:2-53) *by Stephen*
first martyr (7:54-60) *Stephen*
conversion of first "missionary" (9:1-19) *Saul (Paul)*
first Gentile conversion (10:34-48)
first use of the name *Christian* (11:26)
death of the first apostle (12:2)
first missionary call (13:1, 2)
first church council (15:1-30)
first recorded preaching in Europe (16:12, 13)

It is possible to provide a broad general outline for the book, but Luke was obviously not thinking in outlines when he wrote. The book is not a closely reasoned essay, but a loosely knit narrative. You can divide it according to Acts 1:8.

chapters 1-7	Jerusalem
chapter 8	Judea and Samaria
chapters 9-28	to the ends of the earth

But this is too broad. I hope the following summary will be more helpful.

1:1-11. The story begins with Jesus' final instructions to His disciples, then His ascension into Heaven and the promise of His eventual return.

1:12-26. The twelve reconstituted by the election of Matthias to replace Judas. Note Peter's definition of an apostle (vv. 21, 22).

2:1-41. The church is born. God takes the initiative by sending His Holy Spirit, whose miracle of communication prepares for Peter's preaching of the gospel. His sermon is rooted in Scripture, centered on the risen Christ, authenticated by personal testimony (32), and points to Christ's current rule and power. Peter asks for a decision (40). The convinced people repent and are baptized, receiving forgiveness of sins and the gift of the Holy Spirit.

2:42-47. What the new church looks like. The new Christians dedicate themselves to the apostles' teaching, fellowship, breaking of bread, prayers, generosity, and praise. The result is a growing church.

3:1-26. In the name of Jesus, Peter heals a beggar. Having no money, Peter and John do have the power of the name of Jesus. With it they heal a crippled beggar and preach the good news. This compassionate act incites a huge controversy, which lands them in prison.

4:1-37. Peter and John defend themselves and strengthen the believers. When the authorities take note "that these men had been with Jesus," they are helpless. They release them with a warning to "speak no longer to anyone in this name," a promise Peter and John cannot make. The believers rejoice by sharing their possessions.

5:1-11. Hypocrites in the church. Trying to deceive the church, Ananias and Sapphira suddenly die when their sin is uncovered.

5:12-42. We must obey God. Peter and the other apostles are in trouble again for persisting in their preaching. Their only defense against the inevitable growth of opposition is that they must obey God rather than men. They belong to a King above the kings of this world. After a flogging they are released, rejoicing in being considered worthy to suffer shame for Jesus.

6:1-7. The growing church organizes. Unable to do everything themselves, the apostles ask for seven men, traditionally called the first deacons, to assist them. Note the qualifications of these men and compare with today's deacons.

6:8–8:1. Profile of a deacon. Stephen has been chosen from the congregation and given a menial task, but this transformed person does more than is required, even in the face of opposition. He knows his Scriptures and can preach the gospel from them. He looks to Heaven for his reward and rejoices in his suffering.

8:1-8. Nothing can stop the gospel, even persecution. The scattered Christians spread the good news, as the example of Philip demonstrates.

8:9-25. A magician becomes a Christian. Simon the Sorcerer wants the Holy Spirit for base purposes, so he is sternly rebuked by Peter. Simon's repentance is sincere.

8:26-40. A special conversion. Philip explains an Old Testament passage to the traveling Ethiopian court eunuch, then tells him of Jesus and baptizes him.

9:1-31. The conversion of an enemy. From persecutor of Christians to the leading preacher among the Christians, from Saul of Tarsus to Paul the apostle, the change is dramatic. Paul has to overcome his past, change his life-style, and escape his former friends as he strengthens his ties with new friends in the church.

10:1-48. Will God help a person like me? Cornelius is a non-Jewish believer in God. God uses Peter, the prejudiced Jew, to cross over cultural barriers and lead Cornelius to Christ, thus showing that God does not play favorites but that everyone who believes can be saved.

11:1-18. Peter defends himself to his friends. So radical is Peter's departure from Jewish teachings that Peter has to explain that he acted on direct orders from God. The Christians praise God that even Gentiles can be saved.

11:19-30. What are Christians like? Called Christians first in Antioch, the disciples are a talkative, studious, and generous group who are successful in converting to Christ. Barnabas and Saul are prominent leaders there.

12:1-25. Peter lives and Herod dies. Having already killed James, Herod Agrippa arrests Peter, intending to try him after the Passover. But God overrules and sends an angel to arrange Peter's escape. Herod, on the other hand, is later slain by an angel of the Lord and eaten by worms.

13:1–14:28. Paul's missionary journeys begin. The Holy Spirit continues to urge Jesus' disciples on in evangelism, this time by having the Antioch church send Paul and Barnabas on a church-planting mission. Miracles and signs accompany their work. Their strategy in this and subsequent journeys is to head for a major metropolitan area, enter the synagogue, and there try to persuade Jews to accept Christ. Only after Jews reject them do they turn to Gentiles.

15:1-41. The Jerusalem Council. Nothing is more precious to Paul than the unity of all Christians. To be certain that his message to Gentiles is in harmony with what the other apostles and leaders in Jerusalem teach, Paul and his companion, Barnabas, meet with them. The conclusion is a vote of confidence for their ministry.

Following the meeting, Paul begins his next journey without Barnabas, since they cannot agree about John Mark (15:36-41).

15:40–18:22. Paul's second missionary journey. On this journey Paul takes a new companion, Silas. In Lystra they meet

Timothy, a young man whom Paul trains as a preacher. The Holy Spirit alters his plans to preach in Asia; instead he answers the Macedonian call (16:9). In Philippi he converts Lydia and a jailer, who is astounded that Paul and Silas have not escaped during the earthquake. Read the account of his tumultous stay in Thessalonica (17:1-9) and Berea (17:10-15), as well as his unusual sermon to the skeptics in Athens (17:17-34). In the wicked city of Corinth a discouraged Paul, fighting rejection and illness, receives an encouraging word from God: "I am with you." In this city he also enjoys the rich friendship of Aquila and Priscilla.

18:23–20:38. Paul's third missionary journey. This must be a difficult one, since he has to say his farewells at every stop. His purpose in Galatia and Phrygia is to strengthen the believers. At Ephesus he corrects some of Apollos' incomplete teaching (18:24—19:7) but runs into severe hostility during his two-year stay, especially because his preaching is a direct challenge to the followers of the goddess Artemis or Diana. After leaving Ephesus, Paul stays three months in Greece, then returns through Macedonia to Troas, where he raises Eutychus from the dead. Later he meets the Ephesian elders at Miletus.

21:1–24:27. On to Jerusalem and danger. Like Jesus before him, Paul sets his course for Jerusalem fully knowing the dangers that await him there. He is falsely charged with violating the temple and teaching against the Jewish law. With his life in jeopardy, Paul tells his story to the mob (chapter 22), then escapes further danger by claiming the protection of his Roman citizenship. He appears before the Sanhedrin and confounds them (chapter 23); he again escapes death by being transferred to Caesarea, where he is tried before the Roman governor Felix, then kept in limbo for two years.

25:1–28:31. On to Rome. Festus succeeds Felix as governor and hears Paul's appeal to the Emperor. Since King Agrippa and Bernice were visiting Festus, the latter arranges a hearing for their benefit. So once again Paul tells his story (chapter 26). Agrippa's conclusion is that "this man could have been set free, if he had not appealed to Caesar." But to Caesar he has appealed, and to Ceasar he must go.

The final chapters of this exciting drama narrate Paul's narrow escape from shipwreck (chapter 27) and his arrival in Rome, where he continues to preach the kingdom of God and the Lord Jesus Christ as he awaits his trial before Caesar.

Test Your Knowledge

The Book of Acts reveals many of the characteristics of the local church, The following verses help our understanding of the early—and present—church.

1. Believers devoted themselves to _apostles' teaching, fellowship, breaking of bread_, and _prayers_ (2:42).

2. Members _gave_ to anyone in need (2:45).

3. All believers were _one_ in heart and mind (4:32).

4. There were _not_ needy persons among them (4:34).

5. The apostles _did not_ stopped teaching and proclaiming the _Jesus of Christ_ (5:42).

6. To get some assistance, the apostles asked the church to choose _7_ men full of _Spirit_ and _wisdom_. The apostles needed this help so they themselves could give full attention to _prayer_ and the ministry of _the word_ (6:1-4).

7. The persecuted Christians were driven away from Jerusalem, but they _____ the Word _____ they went (8:4).

8. The church was _multiplied_ by the Holy Spirit and lived in _fear_ of the Lord (9:31).

9. God granted _Gentiles_ as well as Jews repentance unto life (11:18).

10. The disciples were first called _Christians_ in Antioch (11:26).

11. It was James' judgment that the church should not make it _trouble_ for Gentiles to turn to God (15:19).

12. The Philippian jailer was told he must _believe_ to be saved. Then he and his family were _baptized_ (16:30-33).

46

13. Church leaders must _____heed_____ the flock as good _____ (20:28).

14. To the very end the apostle Paul boldly preached the kingdom of God and taught about _Lord Jesus Christ_ (28:31).

Letters To Christians of All Nations

Romans and Galatians
Romans 5; Galatians 5

Romans

Author: Paul, writing probably from Corinth around A.D. 58, "to all in Rome who are loved by God and called to be saints" (Romans 1:1, 7).

Theme: "The righteous will live by faith" (1:17).

Characteristics:
1. Longest, most systematic letter of Paul.
2. More like a doctrinal essay than a letter.
3. Written to a church Paul had never visited.
4. Sometimes called the Constitution of Christianity.

The vigorous community of believers in Rome served the Lord in the shadow of the emperor (Nero ruled from A.D. 54 to 68), a circumstance that toughened believers and made their church famous throughout the world for its faith (1:8). From Jerusalem the Christian message had gone out into Judea and Samaria, and now it was even in Rome, the capital of the known world. The church there was made up of Jews, the traditional people of God, and Gentiles, whom the Jews once had disdained as no people at all.

Paul, the apostle to the Gentiles, takes pains in his letter to this mixed congregation to show that Christ has made possible the salvation of both Jews and Gentiles.

Jews were famous in a corrupt world for their slavish obedience to the law of Moses. Yet, as Paul points out, perfect obedience was not attained, even by the Jews. In their hearts Jews were as guilty as Gentiles, and nothing in the law could wash away their guilt. They could really do nothing to earn their salvation—which made them just like Gentiles before God. If there is to be any hope of a right relationship with God, He must make it possible.

Praise God, the exultant apostle exclaims, that is exactly what God has done. Thanks to His *grace,* we can be saved!

But if Paul is right, what shall we say about God's earlier promises to Abraham? Didn't He make Abraham's blood descendants His chosen people? If that is true, and it is, then why didn't the chosen people accept Jesus as the Messiah? Is what Paul preaches about salvation in Christ the truth?

Paul gives a large portion of his argument to these questions (chapters 9-11). He insists that the real descendant of Abraham is not one who can trace his blood lineage back to him, but is instead the one who trusts in God the way Abraham did. Blood descent means nothing; neither does circumcision nor other rites of the law of Moses. The new Israel of God is composed of those who believe as Abraham believed. Since God has now decreed that salvation is through Jesus Christ, Abraham's people are those who obey God in Christ.

In Romans, then, Paul provides the rationale for Jesus' commission to His disciples. If salvation were just for the biological offspring of Abraham, there would be no reason to take the gospel to anybody at all. Only blood would count. But since God is determined to get back what belongs to Him, and since He has made that possible through faith in Jesus, it is imperative that the gospel be preached to everybody everywhere.

We'll trace Paul's argument through the following summary.

Introduction (1:1-17)

Paul identifies himself as a servant of Christ Jesus and an apostle sent to proclaim the gospel of Jesus. Then he offers a word of thanks for the Romans' faith and expresses his longing to visit them in order to encourage them and be encouraged by them. He concludes his introduction with his letter's theme, a now-famous statement drawn from Habakkuk 2:4: "The righteous will live by faith" (Romans 1:17).

What we are without Christ (1:18—3:20)

Paul moves quickly to establish the fact that all men are sinners. They have ignored God, even though He has made it possible for them to know Him. God has abandoned them to their lusts, and their condition is deplorable.

The Jews, long contemptuous of non-Jews, convinced that Israel alone is God's chosen nation, are equally deserving of condemnation. They have abused their privileges and have pursued evil. Even the law about which they boast, but which they regularly disobey, will in the end destroy them. Such is the fate of lawbreakers.

This is not to say that Jews have no advantage. They do, because God has entrusted His words to them, and God is faithful. The fault is not with God, not with the law, but with the sin of which Jews and Gentiles alike are guilty.

What we can become through faith in Christ (3:21—5:21)

The law cannot rescue us from the consequences of our sin, but God's grace can. Believers in Jesus, who embodies God's love toward sinful humanity, "are justified freely by his grace through the redemption that came by Christ Jesus" (Romans 3:24). Paul uses a legal term—*justification*—to picture what God has done for us. We stand accused before the impartial Judge; He knows we are guilty, but because His Son has already paid our penalty, He declares us innocent!

Does this mean that the law was unnecessary? Not at all. But long before the law was given, Abraham "believed God" and therefore was considered a righteous man even though his life was not totally righteous. Likewise we who live after Christ's redeeming act can also be judged righteous through our faith. Abraham continued to hope that what God promised would come true, even when it did not seem possible. He believed that God had the power to give him a son in spite of his and Sarah's advanced age.

Likewise we believe we can be declared innocent by God in spite of our sinful record. God has chosen to save us through Christ; if we accept by faith what He has done for us, we shall have peace with God. That goes for the most ungodly of us! This is all God's doing and not to our credit—but certainly to our benefit. As death came through Adam, life has now come through Jesus.

What is this new life of faith like? (6:1—8:39)

Strange though it sounds, we have been born again. We cannot go on sinning in our old way (even though we may think we somehow get more grace that way), because we are no longer who we were. In our baptism we died and were buried. The person who arose from the watery grave is now united with Christ, alive to God and dead to sin. We used to be slaves of sin; now we are slaves of right living. We give ourselves over to what is holy, like saints; as a result, we are going to live forever (6:23).

If this seems difficult to understand, think about marriage. The law of matrimony is effective only as long as both spouses are alive. When the husband dies, the widow is free from that law and can marry again. In the same way, the law of sin that used to control you is now powerless, since you died and were buried. You are alive only to God through Christ. The struggle you used to have with sin (7:7-25) is over; Christ has rescued you from that sin which leads to death.

So you will not be condemned. Christ has saved you from the law and its consequences. If you belong to Christ, you belong also to righteousness and to God. As His children you will inherit what is His.

Your future is beyond imagining. You may suffer somewhat now, but your sufferings seem like nothing compared with your future joy. The whole created universe suffers with you as it awaits the fulfillment of God's promises. His Spirit helps you in the meantime, interceding for you with God. And in everything, God is working for your good. Nothing, absolutely nothing, can separate you from God.

What about Israel, then? (9:1—11:36)

If these wonderful promises are true, what has happened to God's earlier covenant with Israel? Has God changed His mind? Not at all. He has remained faithful, but Israel has not! Had Israel believed and obeyed God and not rejected His authority, and had the Jews accepted Jesus as God's promised Savior, they would have been saved. But whoever chooses not to believe in Him cannot be saved.

God has not rejected His people. His people have rejected His Son. A new covenant has now succeeded the old, one that fulfills the intent of the old. What God promised Abraham, ("You shall become the father of a great nation") through faith in Jesus Christ

He now has fulfilled. In Christ will all the true Israel of God be saved.

How will you live this life of faith? (12:1—15:13)

As transformed persons! As persons willing to sacrifice yourselves in service to God, not thinking too highly of yourselves, using your God-given gifts in loving one another in every way, overcoming evil with good. Do not rebel against God's appointed authorities and do not withhold from another anything that is His due or that love demands. Do all this because the end is near.

Further, do not use your freedom fully if it causes a weaker Christian to stumble. Don't dispute over sacred days or what to eat. Since we belong to the Lord we must give an accounting to Him and no one else. We'll not judge but will work for peace, the stronger among us bearing with the weaker.

Some concluding personal remarks (15:14—16:27)

Paul's purpose has been to remind his fellow Christians of these important teachings. He wishes to visit the Romans on his way to Spain, but first must go to Jerusalem with an offering for the poor. He requests their partnership in prayer and then sends his final greetings.

Galatians

Author: Paul, "to the churches in Galatia" (Galatians 1:1, 2). Scholars disagree about the time of writing, but most place it between A.D. 50 and 60.

Theme: Freedom in Christ (5:1).

Characteristics:

1. A very personal letter.
2. Urgent concern for Galatian Christians.
3. Anger with teachers of false doctrine.
4. Addressed to a group of churches.
5. Called "the Magna Charta of Freedom From Legalism" and "the Christian Declaration of Independence."

We receive quite a shock in turning from the carefully reasoned essay to the Romans to this fiery, even angry letter to the Galatians. Paul is under attack, and so is his message. He has founded the Galatian churches on the believers' trust in Jesus as the Christ. That trust is being eroded. Enemies of the gospel have infiltrated the churches and, discrediting Paul's apostleship, they have convinced some believers that it is not enough to be simply Christian. They also have to be Jews. Without circumcision and obedience to other prescriptions of the law of Moses, they will be condemned. Christ alone cannot save them. So say the false teachers.

The leisurely discussion and rather lofty tone that characterize Paul's letter to the Romans are missing here. Paul defends himself and Christ with passion. A major difference in the two letters is in his treatment of the law. In Romans, Paul writes of its holiness (7:12), ascribing its failure to the sinfulness of men (8:3). Still he makes it plain that no one can be made righteous by the law (3:20-22). In Galatians he makes this more emphatic. In comparison with the saving gospel, the law is "weak and miserable" (4:9). Christ is the Savior. One who trusts the law for salvation is "alienated from Christ;" he has "fallen away from grace" (5:4). Both Romans and Galatians point out that there can be salvation in spite of one's transgression of the law, but both declare that the law cannot save. Both letters raise this question: How can one come into a right relationship with God (that is, be justified)? Both give the same answer: There is no justification in the law. Faith, not law, justifies. The letters have the same teaching; they differ only in emphasis.

Defending himself as an apostle, Paul soundly criticizes the Judaizers, the Jewish Christians who taught that belief in Christ *and* comformity to Jewish law are both essential for salvation. Paul appeals to the Galatian Christians to hang on to their precious freedom in Christ. He reminds them that Christians are justified by faith (3:6-9), adopted as children of God (4:4-7), and thus made heirs of God's promises to Abraham (3:15-18). Why should they give up everything they have received in Christ and be once again in bondage to the law?

Let's trace Paul's argument:

Introduction (1:1-5)

Paul's urgency rushes him through his greeting. He omits his customary words of thanks for the readers and hurries to launch his theme. His very first words make it clear that he will tolerate no doubt about his authority. He has been sent from Christ himself! His appointment as a servant and witness was announced in his very first encounter with Jesus (Acts 26:16).

53

Paul defends his authority (1:6—2:21)

Refusing to be placed on the defensive, Paul takes the offensive: "If anybody is preaching to you a gospel other than what you accepted, let him be eternally condemned!" (1:9). He can speak so forcefully because he received the gospel directly from Jesus. It is true that he does not qualify as an apostle according to Peter's conditions in Acts 1:21, 22. But if the Lord wants to make an exception in Paul's case, the Lord has the power to do so. Paul has no doubt that what Jesus revealed to him is the true gospel. Further, when Paul later consulted with the leaders of the church in Jerusalem, whose importance the readers of this letter would readily acknowledge, they accepted Paul as a full partner in the ministry of the gospel. So Paul speaks of his message as revealed by Jesus, revolutionary in its effect on Paul himself, and in every way bringing glory to God.

Although Paul is now under attack, he believes his conduct to be more consistent with freedom in Christ than Peter's hypocritical conduct in Antioch was. Peter felt free to eat with Gentiles when there were no other Jews around, but when some conservative Jewish Christians arrived from Jerusalem, he drew back. Since we are "justified by faith in Christ and not by observing the law," Peter should have enjoyed his freedom from Jewish law even in the presence of Jewish critics.

The fact is that the Christian is *in Christ*. When Christ died and was thus finally set free from the law (for no law has power over a dead man), those who have died with Christ (see Romans 6) have also been set free from the law. We now live by faith.

Paul defends his gospel (3:1—4:31)

His good news is that *salvation is now by faith in Christ* (3:1-14). The Holy Spirit was never promised to anyone for obeying the law, but is promised to those who obey Christ (Acts 2:38). Even Abraham was not special to God because he obeyed the law—it had not even been written yet—but because he believed God. Christ rescued us from being cursed by a law whose demands we could never meet. He took the curse upon himself.

Salvation is the result of God's promise, not the law's effectiveness (3:15-22)

God's promise to Abraham was given 430 years before He gave Moses the law. The sacred Abrahamic agreement was never set aside by the law, nor does the law blot out God's promise. The law was an interim arrangement. God's people persisted in being unfaithful to Him, so He had to make provision for guiding them until He would fulfill His promise. Something better would replace the law.

That something better is sonship (3:23—4:7)

The law served as a kind of tutor to get God's people ready for Christ. Until His coming they would not be free, because they were not yet mature enough for responsible freedom. But now that Christ has come, whoever believes and has been baptized into Him has passed from immaturity into freedom, from slavery into sonship. Older categories that separated or classified humanity are now abolished. Every believer in Christ will be treated with all the respect and given all the rights of a legitimate heir, a chosen son.

Why, then, would you give this up and return to a poorer system? (4:8-11)

And why would you turn against me? (4:12-20)

We used to be close, says Paul. Have I alienated you because I have always told you the truth?

And why would you return to salvery in place of sonship? (4:21-31)

You remember that when Sarah was past the age of childbearing, she gave Abraham her handmaiden Hagar so that he could have a son by her (Genesis 16:8). Then later God promised Sarah she would have a son, and she did. Hagar's son Ishmael was the child of a slave, hence always a slave; but Sarah's son Isaac was the child of God's promise, so the legitimate heir of Abraham. You are children of promise also, like Isaac. Treasure your freedom as His children. You are not slaves.

Paul applies the gospel to the life of freedom in four ways (5:1—6:18)

1. *Freedom from legalism (5:1-12).* Adherence to the rules of the law will not gain you anything. "The only thing that counts is faith expressing itself through love." So do not be misled by anyone who would keep you from obeying the truth.

2. *Freedom from self-indulgence (5:13-26).* Do not indulge sinful nature, or you will suffer grave consequences. Instead, let the fruit of the Spirit grow in you.

3. *Freedom to love and serve (6:1-10).* Take care of each other, including those who instruct you in the faith. You will reap what you sow, so do good to all people.

4. *Freedom to be a new creation (6:11-18).* Nothing else matters. For the sake of this new life, "I bear on my body the marks of Jesus."

As Paul wishes his readers the "grace of our Lord Jesus Christ," he summarizes his argument, for throughout his letter he has argued that *grace,* not our own efforts, will finally save us. His argument is complete.

Test Your Knowledge

True—False

1. _____ The church in Rome, like the churches in the province of Galatia, consisted exclusively of persons of the Jewish faith.

2. _____ Salvation depends on God's grace.

3. _____ The real descendants of Abraham are not his blood relatives but those who live by faith as he did.

4. _____ Paul admits that the Jews have an advantage over Gentiles.

5. _____ Justification is a legal term that means we have paid everything we owe, so we can be saved.

6. _____ The way to get more grace is to sin more to be forgiven more.

7. _____ People of Israel are saved by faith in Christ just as other people are.

8. _____ As Christians we are free to do whatever we want to do, no matter what others think.

9. _____ Paul does not agree with teachers who insist that Christians need to conform to the law of Moses.

10. _____ Paul expresses tolerance for those who preach a gospel that is different from his own.

11. _____ Christians are no longer slaves of law or sin, but they are still slaves—their Master is now Christ.

12. _____ If you indulge the cravings of your "flesh," you will suffer grave consequences.

Letters to a Church in Trouble

First and Second Corinthians

Author: The apostle Paul, writing 1 Corinthians from Ephesus and 2 Corinthians from Macedonia around A.D. 55-57, to "the church of God in Corinth" (1 Corinthians 1:1, 2)

Theme verses: 1 Corinthians 15:58; 2 Corinthians 12:9.

Characteristics of 1 Corinthians:

1. Filled with counsel for the local church.

2. Reveals serious problems that confronted the first-century church—and that challenge today's church.

3. Less doctrinal than Romans; contains practical instructions based on sound doctrine.

Characteristics of 2 Corinthians:

1. A warm, personal letter, more revealing of its author than any of his other letters.

2. An appeal for Paul's brothers and sisters in Corinth to remain faithful to Christ and to him.

3. Revelatory of a weak and very human Paul, using himself as an example of how God, through His grace, is able to accomplish His purposes.

The Corinthian church was a flawed community of believers in a seriously troubled city. The average citizen of Corinth would

57

not have admitted his town had problems. He would instead have boasted of the amazing prosperity Corinth gained from its strategic location on the isthmus between the Gulf of Corinth and the Aegean Sea. Cargo-laden ships were portaged across the isthmus in order to avoid the treacherous journey around the southern end of Greece. Corinth grew bloated and sensual with its wealth, indulging itself in its famous athletic series (the Isthmian Games), its theaters, and its "religions."

It was really the last that made Corinth notorious. "Not for every man is a trip to Corinth" was the popular saying, and Corinthians gloried in their reputation as the most immoral inhabitants of the loose Roman empire. Of religions they could boast, for they had them in abundance. Some of them were so depraved that even Rome refused to license them. Presiding over this moral profligacy was the temple of Aphrodite, the goddess of love, towering high above the lower city on the acropolis that rose nearly nineteen hundred feet above the sea. There a thousand temple priestess prostitutes served "worshipers" from land and sea.

To this city, as challenging a field as we could imagine, Paul went alone on his second missionary journey. Knowing no one, he found work in his tentmaking trade with another Jewish tentmaker, Aquila. This man and his wife Priscilla became two of Paul's closest friends. With their help he began forming the nucleus of the Christian Church of Corinth (see Acts 18). After a year and a half there, Paul moved on to further mission endeavors. Priscilla and Aquila left with him, but stayed at Ephesus while he sailed for Caesarea.

In spite of the later ministry of the brilliant Apollos, the church deteriorated badly after Paul left. It was plagued by division, immorality, and heresy till there seemed to be more of Corinth in the church than of the church in Corinth. Some students think Paul may have made a quick journey or two back to Corinth. It was only two hundred fifty miles across the Aegean Sea from Ephesus, where Paul ministered for nearly three years. We can't be sure Paul made the trip, however. What we do know is that he wrote several letters. These we call 1 and 2 Corinthians are probably the second and third of the series. See 1 Corinthians 5:9, which seems to refer to an earlier letter. That earlier letter has been lost. We know about it only from this brief mention in the letter we call 1 Corinthians.

First Corinthians

Introduction (1:1-9)

Following his normal greeting, Paul conforms to the accepted letter-writing custom of his day by speaking a word of thanks for his readers. Note how carefully he words this paragraph, however. He thanks God for enriching the Corinthians and for giving them spiritual gifts. God is faithful, even if the Corinthians are not.

Divisions in the church (1:10—4:21)

Problem: Loyalty to various human leaders—Paul, Apollos, Cephas—has divided the congregation. Some members, perhaps somewhat self-righteously, claim to follow only Christ.

Paul disavows any right to a "loyal following." He appeals to the cross of Christ, not the wisdom of any man, as the true power of the church. The cross may seem foolish to Greeks and offensive to Jews; but it is the result of God's foolishness, which is wiser than any human wisdom.

Loyalty to any person can lead to hostility and division. Divine wisdom, revealed through the Holy Spirit, is needed for salvation. Truly spiritual members of the church must be weaned from a diet of milk and be ready to receive the meat of solid spiritual nurture. After all, Paul and Apollos are only men. Each makes his contribution to the church, but neither is worthy of partisan support. Paul started the church (as a gardener plants a seed or a builder lays a foundation), and others worked to nourish and build it. But its progress really is due to God. Part of Paul's message may be paraphrased thus:

"We are really servants, anyway, trying to be faithful to what God has given us. Since you cannot see with God's all-knowing eyes, do not judge among us. Do not presume to be better than your teachers. Do not persist in flaunting your arrogance. I am coming to see you, either with a whip or with a gentle spirit. You may choose which."

Solution: Paul offers several antidotes for the poison of division—

1. Remember the message of the cross (1:18-25).
2. Remember what God has done for you (1:26-31).
3. Rest your faith on God's wisdom and power (2:1-16).
4. Build on Jesus Christ, the foundation (3:11).
5. Boast no more about any man (3:1-23).

6. Remember the teachings you received from us (4:1-7).
7. And be humble! (4:8-21).

Immorality in the church (5:1-13)

Problem: Immorality of a kind that would be a disgrace even among pagans! A man living illicitly with his stepmother! And the church winks at it!

Solution: Get rid of the wicked man to keep the church from being destroyed. Don't associate with sexually immoral persons in the church. By your stern action God may be able to save this man's spirit.

Lawsuits among Christians (6:1-11)

Problem: You are actually going to an ungodly judge to settle your disputes! You, who are supposed to judge the world one day! You are disgracing the church before unbelievers.

Solution: Allow yourselves to be cheated before you do anything to bring discredit to the church. Do not adopt the ways of the wicked who will be barred from the kingdom of God.

Sexual Immorality, part two (6:12-20)

Problem: Paul returns to the problem of 5:1-12. Although Christians enjoy incredible freedom in Christ, not everything they *can* do *should* they do.

Solution: Remember that your bodies as well as your spirits belong to Christ. Be united with Him and never with a prostitute. Your body is the Spirit's temple. Honor God with your body.

Carrying Freedom Too Far (8:1—11:1)

Problem: Meat in the Corinthian markets more than likely came from animals that had been used as sacrifices to heathen gods or goddesses. Thrifty priests used only a small portion for the offering; the rest was sold to butcher shops. The question for conscientious Christians was this: If I eat meat that has been offered to an idol, will someone watching me think that I really believe in that god? Will I bring shame to the church?

At first this section seems to have little to do with modern Christians, since we don't face the problem of whether or not to eat food that has been offered to idols. But don't dismiss this discussion too soon. The real issue is not what to eat, but how far to carry our freedom in Christ.

Solutions: Paul answers in several ways.

1. Since an idol represents a god that really does not exist, it does not matter whether we eat or don't eat.

2. Not everybody knows that idols are nothing. Some may be upset by your eating (and maybe even think you are sinning). Then for the sake of your weaker brother, refrain from eating the questionable meal.

3. Paul uses himself as an example. He does not refer again to the eating of meat, since he has said enough on that subject. He talks instead of whether he should take a salary as a preacher. He has every right to receive money from the Corinthians for his service, but he has not used this right. In this matter as in everything else, "I have become all things to all men so that by all possible means I might save some." This is the overriding concern: the saving of others. To that end Paul sternly disciplines himself ("I beat my body and make it my slave") so that he as well as those to whom he preaches will win the prize the gospel awards.

4. Paul then gives a warning from Israel's history. If he, Paul, was an example of selflessness for the sake of others, the Israelites were an example of selfishness. Not even Moses could keep them from idolatry, immorality, or grumbling. So they died in the desert.

5. In conclusion, Paul repeats his main point: An idol is nothing, so you can eat whatever you want to. But remember that you are the body of Christ, as your participation in communion shows. Be faithful to Christ then, and avoid any appearance of belief in demons. You can do anything you want to, but remember that not everything you can do is beneficial or constructive. Live for the good of others and the glory of God.

Abusing Christian Worship (11:2—14:40)

Problem: Remember Corinth's reputation? In a town overrun with religions, many of them nothing more than excuses for immorality, the church has to be doubly careful not to do anything in worship that can be misunderstood by nonbelievers. But the Corinthian Christians are not being careful. To correct several abuses Paul offers the following.

Solutions:

1. Women, conduct yourselves with the propriety expected of the female sex in your culture. Remember your position and the

rules of etiquette. In Galatians 3:28 Paul teaches that in Christ there is neither male nor female; these distinguishing categories have been abolished *in Christ*. But not *in Corinth*. Paul has been arguing against eating meat offered to idols or claiming one's salary as a minister, not because it is wrong, but because it might be misunderstood. Now he applies the same reasoning to the question of women's freedom in worship. Since in the Lord men and women are not independent of each other, let them relate to one another in worship as seems proper, without contention.

2. Let unity, not disunity, be expressed as you participate in the Lord's Supper. You have been rude to one another, the rich eating wtih the rich and ignoring the poor. You have eaten and drunk to excess. (A common meal was enjoyed along with what we call "communion.") Remember that this is the Lord's body and blood! Do not partake "in an unworthy manner"—that is, "without recognizing the body of the Lord." If you think of the bread and the fruit of the vine merely as physical food and drink, of course that is unworthy. But if you partake without regard to the needs of your brothers and sister in Christ, that too is unworthy. We share one bread because we are one body (10:17). If you disregard other members of the body, you bring judgment upon yourselves by this abuse.

3. As you boast of your various "spiritual gifts," remember that there is only one Spirit—the one who enables you to say and *mean,* "Jesus is Lord"—and God gives gifts of the Spirit to individuals for the sake of the group. That is because the church is the body of Christ, one unit made up of many parts, with each part working for the good of the whole. Whatever your gift, use it for the whole body.

4. The most excellent gift of all is the gift of love. You may speak in tongues, or prophesy, or have amazing knowledge or faith; you may even impoverish or martyr yourself; but if you have no love, you have nothing and have done nothing. Love is the mark of the mature Christian. This is the *one* most important gift of all.

5. With that in mind, use whatever other gift you have with love. Speaking specifically of the gift of tongues, since it benefits the speaker but no one else, it is not as helpful a gift as prophecy, which builds others up. Paul can speak in tongues, but says it is far more important to speak "five intelligible words to instruct others than ten thousand words in a tongue."

6. Let your worship be orderly, "for God is not a God of disorder but of peace." Let the men do the leading, as this too is a mark of good order.

Doubting the Resurrection (15:1-58)

Problem: Corinthian Christians have come from a variety of religious backgrounds, with all sorts of ideas about the future life—including the belief that there is none. To Paul this is heretical thinking, since the gospel itself is unthinkable without the resurrection of Jesus Christ.

Solutions:

1. Paul reminds them of the essence of Christian faith, the good news of Jesus, from which Jesus' resurrection cannot be excluded.

2. Then he uses himself as an example again. Would he have preached so fervently, running the risk of heresy, unless he were totally convinced of the truth of the resurrection? He would be a false witness unless Christ had arisen. Although some say categorically, "There is no resurrection," the fact of Jesus' resurrection destroys the category. Facts are facts, in spite of your prejudices!

3. When asked, "How are the dead raised?" one can use the analogy of a seed that dies in order to become something better. God will supply the resurrection body, exchanging our perishable earthly one for an imperishable Heavenly one. Spiritual body will replace physical body. As we resemble Adam physically, so we will resemble Christ spiritually. What is important is that we will be raised and changed, and death will be defeated.

4. In light of this great promise, "let nothing move you. Always give yourselves fully to the work of the Lord."

Closing Comments (16:1-24)

Paul offers practical instructions for sharing money with others, specifically the poor Christians in Jerusalem. He then tells of his future plans, commends Timothy and others to the Corinthians, and sends his final greetings.

Second Corinthians

Second Corinthians seems to have been written swiftly out of a heart overflowing with joy and love mingled with sorrow and some indignation. It is not easy to make a formal outline, but we can see that Paul has several purposes in mind. Some of them are defensive, for his apostolic authority is under attack in Corinth. Paul rapidly:

1. Presents the purposes of his sufferings in Asia (1:3-11).
2. Explains his change of plans for a return visit (1:12—2:4).
3. Instructs the Corinthians concerning the disciplining and reconciling of an offender (see 1 Corinthians 5) (2:5-11).
4. Shows that the ministry of grace is superior to the ministry of law (2:12—6:13).
5. Orders separation from false teachers (6:14—7:1).
6. Expresses his joy over the Corinthians' revival (7:2-16).
7. Urges the church to complete its collection (8:1—9:15).
8. Defends his apostleship against charges of false apostles (10:1—13:14).

Paul does not feel comfortable in talking so much about himself. Over and over again he blushes, "I am speaking as a fool" (11:1, 17, 21). His self-consciousness is part of the letter's appeal, however, exposing the very human side of this complex man. He suffers, he hurts, he cares, he cries, he gives everything he has for his ministry. He anguishes over the charges of his critics and over the damage they are doing to his beloved church. He does not write as an authoritative apostle so much as the spiritual father of these young Christians in Corinth whom he loves and wants to be loved by.

Comfort (1:3-11)

In place of his usual words of thanksgiving for those to whom he is writing, Paul thanks God for His never-failing comfort in time of trouble. Notice how frequently he repeats the word *comfort,* which means "to strengthen with." Paul's sufferings have been for the Corinthians' comfort and to help him rely more completely on God.

Merciful Change (1:12—2:4)

In light of Paul's total reliance upon God, his critics are ill-advised to accuse him of being fickle because he had to change his plans to visit Corinth. "God is faithful and so am I," he tells the Corinthians. Having said "yes" to Christ once, trusting in the one who is always trustworthy (whose "Yes" can be counted on), he still trusts Him. God will testify that Paul is steadfast and that his failure to come to Corinth as planned was for the Corinthians' sake.

Forgiveness (2:5-11)

Now that the offender (1 Corinthians 5) has been punished, you must love and forgive. You have proved your willingness to obey me; now reach out to the offender in forgiveness.

The Ministry of Grace (2:12—6:13)

Expressing disappointment in not finding Titus in Troas, Paul launches a discussion of his ministry, which includes some of his finest writing. His is a ministry with a difference. Refusing to be like others who preach for money, Paul has effectively shared the gospel. Proof of his effectiveness is the Corinthian Christians; they are his "letters of recommendation." Having no special skills of their own, Paul and his colleagues can boast of God's work through them in teaching a new agreement between God and man, the covenant that Christ delivered. Theirs is a ministry of the Holy Spirit, proclaiming Christ, and not the ministry of the law. The ministry of the Spirit frees from the shackles of the law.

Preachers are flawed, of course, holding the wealth of the gospel as an earthen pot contains treasures. You admire the treasure, not the pot; pay attention to the message, not the flawed messengers. We preach Christ, not ourselves. Fix your eyes, therefore, on the eternal.

Our bodies are weak and dying, like tents that deteriorate with time. But our destiny is to dwell in "an eternal house in heaven." We are burdened here, but hereafter we shall live free of burdens. That is why our only concern is to please Him who will grant us this eternal home.

In the meantime we dwell on earth, compelled by Christ's love (the Christ who died for all) to preach the good news that everyone may become more than human, a new creation in Christ. Through Christ God was making friends again with those who had sinned against Him. We preachers, then, are Christ's ambassadors to beg you to be reconciled to God—right now. We'll do nothing to hinder anyone from coming to Christ. We'll endure everything rather than bring shame to this ministry.

Purity (6:14—7:1)

Paul turns now from the defense of his ministry to his appeal for purity in the congregation. Since the church is the temple of the living God, it must be holy. Let there be no unbelievers, no wickedness, no darkness, and no idolatry in the church. Be pure!

65

Joy Out of Sorrow (7:2-16)

Paul's earlier letter brought sorrow to the Corinthians, and he was sorry about that. But their sorrow caused them to repent, and that brought him overflowing joy. They are turning to the purity advocated in 6:14—7:1.

Money Raising (8:1—9:15)

One of Paul's paramount concerns as he travels from church to church is the destitute condition of the Christians in Jerusalem. He intends to carry a large offering to them soon. He urges the Corinthians to give generously, following the example of the churches at Philippi and elsewhere in Macedonia. They did not use their poverty as an excuse, but gave with amazing generosity. Paul's principle is that of equality: those who have should not have too much while those with little have too little.

Titus is helping Paul with the offering. The Corinthians should receive him and his partners with a warm welcome.

Paul has already boasted of their generosity to others. He appeals to them not to disappoint him. Urging them to sow generously so they may reap generously, he reminds them that they cannot count on God to provide what they need in order to give cheerfully.

Self Defense (10:1—13:14)

Paul returns to his defense of his ministry, affirming his apostolic authority and denying that of the false teachers who are confusing the Corinthians. He insists he belongs to Christ, in whom alone he will boast.

Paul may not be an impressive speaker, but he knows Christ. He has preached freely, taking no pay, that he will not be identified with those who preach for the money they can get.

Paul's pay has not been money but suffering, both physical and mental. He is weak, but his weakness is not to be held against him. It is his very weakness that is God's opportunity, for God's "power is made perfect in weakness." Paul may have wronged them in not allowing them to help support him, but he showed among them the marks of an apostle—"signs, wonders and miracles"—in addition to his teaching. When he comes a third time he will still take nothing from them. His concern remains the same: "Everything we do, dear friends, is for your strengthening."

With some final warnings Paul brings this amazing letter to a close. "Our prayer is for your perfection."

Test Your Knowledge

From the list of chapters at the bottom, select the proper one for each of the following:

1. _____ The love chapter.
2. _____ A discussion of the Christian's freedom to eat whatever he wants.
3. _____ Paul's boast about his sufferings.
4. _____ A comparison of God's foolishness with man's wisdom.
5. _____ Paul's teaching on marriage.
6. _____ An appeal for money.
7. _____ A discussion of speaking in tongues.
8. _____ A case of gross immorality in the church.
9. _____ A discussion of the Lord's Supper.
10. _____ Praises of the comfort that comes from God to those who need it.

a) 1 Corinthians 1
b) 1 Corinthians 5
c) 1 Corinthians 7
d) 1 Corinthians 8
e) 1 Corinthians 10, 11

f) 1 Corinthians 13
g) 1 Corinthians 14
h) 2 Corinthians 1
i) 2 Corinthians 8, 9
j) 2 Corinthians 11

handwritten notes: Eph 1:9-10 3:2-6 6:19

Letters That Plead for Unity

Ephesians, Colossians, Philemon
Ephesians 1:9, 10; 4:1-16
Colossians 1:15-20

Ephesians and Colossians are enough alike to be called twin epistles. Written about the same time, they have striking similarities. Of the 155 verses in Ephesians, the content of 78 is repeated in Colossians, with over 55 verses being verbatim. These two letters were written about the same time, and both were sent to churches in the province called Asia. Both include some of Paul's most exalted writing on the majesty of Christ.

Paul is writing to churches wracked by discord. Strange doctrines have threatened to undo the good work of the gospel. Appealing for unity, Paul reminds his readers that Christ is without equal. He alone unites all persons and indeed all reality in himself. In Colossians Paul lifts up the *person* of Christ as the all-sufficient Lord of the universe: in Ephesians he exalts the *body* of Christ, the church, as evidence of God's desire for unity in the world.

Ephesians

Author: Paul, writing probably from Rome A.D. 62 or 63, to the churches at Ephesus and elsewhere in Asia. (For information on Paul's Ephesian ministry, see Acts 18:18-21; 19:1-41; 20:17-38.)

Theme: The unity of all things in Christ, and the church as symbol of that unity (1:22, 23).

Characteristics:
1. Several of Paul's greatest themes are included here:
   Justification by grace through faith (2:4-10)
   Work of the Holy Spirit (1:13, 14; 2:18, 22; 3:16-19)
   The Christian *in Christ* and Christ *in the Christian.*
   The Church
     Christ's Body (1:22, 23; 2:16; 4:4, 12, 16)
     Household of God (2:19)
     Building (2:21)
     Holy Temple in the Lord (2:21)
     Habitation of God (2:22)
     Children of God (5:1)
     Children of Light (5:8)
2. An impersonal letter, lacking Paul's usual personal greetings.
3. Carefully reasoned, a well-developed essay.
4. Generally divided into three chapters of doctrine and three of practical application, although doctrine and application are intermingled throughout.

In Ephesians Paul discusses the *Wealth,* the *Walk,* and the *Warfare* of the Christian.

The Christian's Wealth (1:1—3:21)
Count the blessings Paul mentions in the first full paragraph (1:3-10). We are blessed

in Christ
  in being chosen to be holy and blameless
    in our adoption as sons
      in our redemption
        in our forgiveness of sins
          in receiving God's lavish grace
            in knowing the mystery of God's will, which is "to bring all things in heaven and on earth together under one head, even Christ."

Paul says God gives all these blessings so that we (Jews) and you (Gentiles) may together be for the praise of his glory (1:11-14). We who have received so much ought to praise Him.

Now let's paraphrase and condense the rest of Paul's words to the end of chapter 3.

1:15-23

I [Paul] pray that you may be given knowledge to go with your faith, so that you will really know the richness of your riches and the unparalleled power of Christ.

2:1-10

You and I were dead when we were outside of Christ, slaves to the passions and powers of this world. You can't exist for yourself (your human nature) alone and really live. We need to have Christ make us alive through our faith in Him. Now that we are *in* Christ we *are* alive!

2:11-22

So far I have spoken of you (uncircumcised Gentiles) and us (circumcised Jews). In truth, however, such distinctions are meaningless in Christ, who has brought us together. He is our peacemaker. If you are in Christ and so am I, we are one. We are equal citizens in the church God has built on Christ.

3:1-21

I have my ministry because the Holy Spirit revealed to me this mystery of God's desire to treat both Gentiles and Jews as equal heirs and sharers of every good in Christ Jesus. I don't deserve to be a minister of the gospel, of course, but God's grace has made it possible for me. He has sent me to you Gentiles so that you too may hear what I have heard and be free to approach God with confidence.

So I pray for you to the Father who unites us all. May you be strengthened by the Holy Spirit and by Christ so that you may be filled with God!

You are rich!

The Christian's Walk (4:1—6:9)

The Christian's walk, of course, includes all that he does. It is his whole way of living.

4:1-6

Endowed with all the wealth described above, Christians should walk like Christians, not hoarding their riches to themselves, but living a life worthy of their high calling. The Christian has been given his legacy so that he can help the church do its work. Since a united church is Exhibit A of God's desire to unite everything in Christ, it cannot be divided. There is just "one body and one Spirit."

4:7-16

The church's ministry is the same as Christ's. Christ's gifts to the church are persons (apostles, prophets, and so on) who equip church members to build up the entire body to express its unity in belief and action. The true church will not divide over strange or deceptive teachings. It will not be led astray as children often are. The body will be one, held together by truth and love.

4:17–5:20

Only the highest ethical conduct can maintain this precious but fragile unity. Since God has given new life to those in Christ, they must never return to their former unenlightened behavior. They have left behind them forever all lies, unchecked anger, theft, unwholesome talk, bitterness, and other disruptive conduct. Now they imitate God, in whom there is no immorality or greed or idolatry or darkness. They walk carefully, but with singing and thanksgiving in their hearts.

5:21–6:9

Harmonious personal relationships are achieved through mutual submission. Neither the wife nor the husband can lord it over the spouse. Every selfish desire is subordinated to the good of the partner. Children obey their parents, who in turn think and act for the good of their children. Slaves (employees) do not cheat their masters (employers), but neither are masters (bosses) guilty of neglecting the welfare of their workers. All relationships are conducted in a way that evidences the new life in Christ.

The Christian's Warfare (6:10-24)

It isn't easy to leave one's past or to battle one's present temptations. Only in the strength of the Lord is victory possible. Our battle is not just against flesh and blood (other persons or our own human desires). It is against ideas, attitudes, dictates of culture; and it is against unseen powers, spirits, and mighty forces that war against God's will. The Christian can win—but only in the Lord's strength and the armor He provides.

Even I, Paul, need help. So pray for me.

71

Colossians

Author: Paul, writing probably from Rome, around A.D. 62 or 63, to the church at Colosse, a city in Asia. (We have no knowledge that Paul started this church; perhaps someone he influenced during his Ephesian ministry was responsible.)

Theme: The incomparable Christ, in whom "all things hold together" (1:15-20).

Characteristics:

1. Similar to Ephesians in theme and development.

2. Differs from Ephesians in specifically dealing with problems in one church.

3. Like Ephesians, written primarily to Gentile Christians.

The problems in the Colossian church were intellectual. Central Asia Minor was not only hospitable to the gospel of Christ, but also was fertile territory for a host of religions, especially those appealing to human vanity. It is not flattering to be told that God stooped to the lowest human level in order to save everybody, even the illiterate peasant. A heaven populated with everybody from everywhere is not very appealing to someone who thinks himself a somebody! It is not hard to understand why certain Christians easily succumb to the snobbish appeal of Gnosticism.

Gnosticism is a large word that covers a multitude of heresies. Its root means "knowing," and it suggests that Gnostics are those "in the know." Gnostics liked to believe that they alone, the "knowing ones," could be saved.

Further, this religion of the mind held that mind (or spirit) is good, but matter is evil. Since God is good, He must be spirit only. In the Gnostics' opinion He could not possibly live in a human body, for such a body is material and therefore evil. Some Gnostics did indeed say the divine Spirit came to Jesus when He was baptized and departed when He died; but the more general opinion was that Jesus' body was a phantasm, an illusion, and not a material body at all.

This strange doctrine had its effects on Christian behavior, too. It led some to asceticism. They said the evil flesh must be deprived of pleasure and completely subjugated to the spirit through religious rites, legal regulations, dietary laws, circumcision, and so on. But the same doctrine led others to sensual abandonment. Since the flesh is evil and only the spirit is good, they said, it doesn't matter what the body does. It may as well be allowed to indulge in anything that seems pleasant.

Paul has his hands full in refuting this heresy. In the Corinthian letters Paul defends himself from his critics' charges; but in Colosse Christ himself is under attack. This letter is Paul's defense, not of himself this time, but of his Lord. Let us briefly summarize what he says.

1:1-14

May God give you true knowledge, wisdom, understanding, and a life worthy of the Lord! He has qualified you already to share in the inheritance of the saints in light. You need no higher knowledge!

1:15-20

Jesus is all you need, period! He is no *creature* of God like us, but is instead—and here Paul's vocabulary soars—"the image of the invisible God, the firstborn over all creation." He is the Creator, the preeminent one, the head of the church, the first resurrected one, the one in whom God dwelt fully and through whom God is bringing everything together. Thus in one paragraph Paul has answered the Gnostics.

1:21–2:5

Further, you who read this letter are proof that God has brought man into a closer relationship with Him through Christ's death. And I, Paul, am a preacher of this good news. To preach this truth I have suffered for you, wanting to present you perfect in Christ, who alone is your hope.

2:6-23

Enjoy your freedom in Christ. Get your strength from Christ and not from empty human speculation. In Christ God lives bodily, and in you Christ dwells. You have the true circumcision—not in flesh, but in cutting off the rule of your human nature when you died with Christ in baptism. Once you were dead in sin, but now you are alive in Him, forgiven, free from obligations to anybody's religious rituals or holy days. Don't worship angels, but the one over angels; don't worry about the rules of others in this world. They will perish; live for the eternal one.

Enjoy your life in Christ. Concentrate on the holy and eternal; no longer allowing "whatever belongs to your earthly nature" to control you. Replace dark actions and motives like immorality, lust, greed, anger, slander, and filthy language with actions befitting God's chosen people, bathing everything in the qualities of love. Let your life together in church be ruled by the peace of Christ as His Word dwells in you richly through teaching and singing with thanksgiving.

Let Christ rule in your social relationships also at home and at work as you submit to one another for His sake. Be devoted to prayer—and include us as you pray. Be wise in every way.

4:7-18

Tychicus, who is carrying this letter to you [and the letters to the Ephesians and to Philemon] will give you further personal news.

My fellow prisoner Aristarchus and others with me join in sending greetings.

Grace be with you.

Philemon

Ephesians and Colossians appeal for the unity of all Christians in Christ. Paul includes the practical suggestion that the way to achieve harmony is through mutual submission—husband to wife, wife to husband; parents to children, children to parents; slaves to masters, masters to slaves. Philemon reads like a case study of the mutual submission Paul is pleading for in the other letters. Paul wrote this short note to Philemon toward the end of his Roman imprisonment, about the time of Ephesians and Colossians.

Onesimus, Philemon's slave, had fled from his master to Rome, where he somehow came under Paul's influence. As we would expect, Paul led him to Christ. The two became fast friends in the Lord. Their companionship could not last indefinitely, however, Onesimus was Philemon's legal property. Paul had to return him to his owner. Since Tychicus was carrying his letters to Ephesus and Colosse, Paul asked Tychicus to take Onesimus along.

Modern readers of this letter are often amazed that Paul does not set Onesimus free or instruct Philemon to do so. Nowhere, in fact, does the Bible directly attack the institution of slavery.

However, Philemon and other Scriptures certainly appeal for humane treatment of slaves. This letter goes even further. It offers a higher principle by which slaveholders would naturally be moved to release their slaves, if such release would be for the good of the slave. In Christ there is neither Jew nor Gentile, slave nor free, male nor female (Galatians 3:28). Consistent with that teaching, Paul now tells Philemon that he should receive Onesimus "no longer as a slave, but better than a slave, as a dear brother" (16).

Paul takes another unusual step. Having (1) sent the slave back to slavery and (2) urged his owner to receive him with full forgiveness and as an equal in Christ, he now (3) offers to reimburse Philemon for anything Onesimus owes his master, even though of course Paul is under no obligation whatever. In making this offer, Paul is acting toward Onesimus as Christ has acted toward us—he is taking upon himself someone else's obligation. This is Christian brotherhood at its best. It is the way to destroy slavery—and to achieve unity.

In the second century the prominent Christian writer Ignatius mentions one Onesimus, the bishop of Ephesus. It is tempting—though unprovable—to think the bishop may have been this same runaway slave.

Test Your Knowledge

1. Why are Ephesians and Colossians called twin epistles?

2. What makes us "fellow citizens with God's people," regardless of our backgrounds?

3. The church's ministry is the same as Christ's. What then is the church supposed to be doing?

4. What is the relationship between high ethical conduct and the unity of Christians?

5. In what way is the husband the head of the wife?

6. Can you give a definition of Gnosticism? Do you see any evidences that it is still around today?

7. Reread Colossians 1:15-20 and describe Christ in your own words.

8. What is the true circumcision?

9. Could you have done what Paul asked Philemon to do—accept Onesimus without any punishment or rebuke?

10. Should Paul have offered to pay Philemon money? Would you have?

Letters to Greece

Philippians and 1 and 2 Thessalonians
Philippians 4:4-7, 10-13;
1 Thessalonians 4:13-18; 5:1-11

"Come over to Macedonia and help us." This famous "Macedonian call" came to Paul in a vision when he and his traveling companions were in Troas (Acts 16:9). They had not planned to travel to Macedonia, but now they did.

In the fourth century B.C. the little country of Macedonia began to dominate its world. Alexander the Great consolidated the military gains of his father Philip and then marched his armies forth to win the rest of the Mediterranean nations. He was after more than military conquest. He carried his country's culture and language with him and was so successful a missionary that centuries later, when Rome ruled politically, Greek language and culture overruled. If the gospel could take root in Macedonia as well as Rome, it would be in a strategic position to influence people wherever Greek was spoken.

It is no wonder that Paul so quickly obeyed his vision. Before long Philippi (named after Alexander's father) and Thessalonica (named for his half-sister), and later Athens and Corinth (in southern Greece), had heard about Jesus.

Philippians

Author: Paul, writing from prison in Rome about A.D. 63 to his close friends in the church at Philippi.

76

Theme: The letter is not characterized so much by a theme as by the joyful tone that rings throughout. It is the epistle of joy.

This buoyant personal letter, perhaps the last of Paul's letters to churches, defies formal outlining. It is not that kind of letter. The writer is not dealing with weighty doctrinal matters, as in Romans, nor is he answering a letter or trying to solve some problems, as in his Corinthian correspondence. He writes instead to inform his friends of his present condition in prison. He doesn't want them to worry about him. Appealing as always for unity in Christ, he urges them to imitate the example Christ set on the cross. Such humility is the best possible way to preserve peace in the church.

Paul also warns his friends against those poisonous infiltrators, the Judaizers, who would force every Christian to conform to the rules of Judaism as well as the teachings of Christ. Then he gives them additional spiritual instructions. Through it all, he rejoices in his victory over the chains that hold him.

The church he loves is the embodiment of unity in diversity. It is a cosmopolitan group, including at least one wealthy woman, Lydia, the merchant in whose house the church meets (Acts 16:12-15, 40), a jailer and his family (Acts 16:16-34), probably the slave girl for whose rescue Paul and Silas were imprisoned, and perhaps some of their fellow prisoners. The young church has kept in close touch with Paul during his subsequent ministries, sending gifts to Thessalonica (Philippians 4:14-16; Acts 17:1-9), exchanging messages through other Christian workers, and enjoying Paul's later visits to them (Acts 20:1-6).

The immediate occasion of the letter is this: News of Paul's imprisonment has come to the church at Philippi. Concerned for Paul's welfare, the members dispatch Epaphroditus to carry their gifts of money and love to him. Upon arriving, Epaphroditus sees that Paul's situation is not good, so he decides to stay with him, perhaps working to earn more money for Paul's and his own needs. While there he becomes very ill and almost dies. Word of his sickness somehow reaches Philippi. When Epaphroditus learns that they are aware of his condition, he worries that they will now add their worries for him to their worries about Paul. Paul sends him back to Philippi as soon as he is able to go. This letter is in Epaphroditus' hand when he is reunited with his Christian brothers and sisters in Philippi.

To summarize the letter we'll borrow sectional headings from the New International Version. After the usual greetings, Paul offers the following.

Thanksgiving and Prayer (1:3-11)
Memorize the opening words. You'll use them often: "I thank my God every time I remember you." The rest of the letter is equally affectionate.

Paul's Chains Advance the Gospel (1:12-30)
I [Paul] rejoice because I know that even in prison the cause to which I have given my life is being helped. My guards are learning of Jesus, and my fellow Christians outside are being encouraged. For this reason I am torn between wanting to live and serve the Lord and wanting to die and be with Him. No matter what the Roman authorities decide to do with me, I will be content. So must you be, always standing firm in your faith.

Imitating Christ's Humility (2:1-11)
Christ is the supreme example of humility in the service of God. God has therefore exalted Him, but He never exalted himself. Nor should we ever strive for self-glory. We need to have the mind of Christ.

Shining as Stars (2:12-18)
In complete obedience to God, be pure and blameless children of God—shining like stars in the universe. Even if I am sacrificed, "you too should be glad and rejoice with me."

Timothy and Epaphroditus (2:19-30)
I hope to send Timothy to you soon. He loves you and wants only the best for you. Epaphroditus is carrying this letter. I want you to know how sacrificially he has served me. Welcome him with honor, for he deserves it, having almost died in helping me.

No Confidence in the Flesh (3:1-11)
Beware of anyone who teaches you to put your faith in circumcision or other acts of the law. I used to do so myself, but every good thing I did or gained I now realize was worthless when compared with what I have gained in Christ. Only in Him is resurrection possible.

Pressing on Toward the Goal (3:12—4:1)

The blessings to be gained in Christ are so great that I am not content to rest on anything I have already done. I'm like an athlete straining to win the prize. Do the same—not like people whose god is the stomach, but as citizens of Heaven itself, where Christ will tranform us into His likeness.

Exhortations (4:2-9)

Christians—especially you, Euodia and Syntyche—must be of one spirit in the church. All of you should rejoice in the Lord with gentleness and an absence of anxiety. Keep thinking the highest thoughts and practicing the virtues I have taught you. God will give you peace.

Thanks for Their Gifts (4:10-20)

I appreciate what you have done for me, even though I want you to know I have learned either to do with or to do without; I can be poor or rich. God provides the strength for me to do everything. But it was good of you to share my troubles. Your gifts are like a fragrant offering to God. As He has met my needs, so will He meet all of yours.

Final Greeting (4:21-23)

To all the saints (Christians) in Christ, the grace of the Lord Jesus Christ be with your spirit.

First and Second Thessalonians

Author: Paul, from Corinth, about A.D. 51 or 52, to the church in Thessalonica.

Theme: If one theme can be singled out, it is the second coming of Christ.

Characteristics: Early letters, written shortly after Paul established the church there. The second follows the first by only a few months.

According to Acts 17:1-10, Paul had an amazingly short ministry of three weeks in Thessalonica, yet in this brief time he founded a church. His success aroused the jealousy of Jewish leaders who drove him out of town and, when they learned of Paul's subsequent success in Berea, pursued him there and incited mobs against him. Fleeing Berea, Paul stayed briefly in Athens. It was from there that he sent Timothy back to look after the Thessalonians while he himself went on to Corinth (1 Thessalonians 3:1, 2)

At Corinth Timothy rejoined him (Acts 18:5), carrying encouraging reports that the Thessalonians were steadfast in their love of Paul and their faith in Christ (1 Thessalonians 3:6). In a happy mood, then, Paul quickly wrote and dispatched a letter commending them for their faith and updating them on his activities. He also dealt with some of the moral and doctrinal problems that Timothy reported had crept into the fellowship.

First Thessalonians

1:1–2:16

As usual, Paul follows his greetings with words of thanksgiving for the Thessalonians' faith, a faith known not only in Greece (Macedonia and Achaia) but everywhere among Christians. He then reflects on his successful ministry among them, when he and his colleagues preached Christ only, supporting themselves so that they would work no hardship on the believers. And believers they were. Becoming "imitators of God's churches in Judea," they were even given the privilege of suffering as the Christians in Judea did.

2:17—3:13

Longing to see them again but prevented by Satan, Paul has earlier sent Timothy to encourage them. Timothy has brought back an encouraging report of their steadfastness. This word has added to Paul's desire to see them.

4:1-12

As in his presence, so now in this letter Paul encourages them to live to please God in holiness and brotherly love, living a quiet life that earns the respect of outsiders.

4:13-18

Nearing the end of his letter, Paul introduces a subject that he has learned is troubling the young Christians: the second coming of the Lord. It seems that the Thessalonians have been worrying about those who have died. Some Thessalonians may even have stopped working to wait for the Lord's expected return. To ease their anxiety—and to get them working again—Paul sends these comforting words. Those who are dead will rise when Jesus returns. Together with those who have not died they will meet the Lord in the clouds of heaven.

5:1-11

It is vain to speculate "about times and dates," since "the day of the Lord will come like a thief in the night." Christians are children of the day—living holy and controlled lives—so they do not need to fear when He comes. They will be ready to receive salvation.

5:12-28

Paul's letter draws to a close with some final instructions to respect those who work and oversee, to be at peace with one another, to be joyful, praying, giving thanks in every circumstance, remaining faithful as God is faithful.

Second Thessalonians

Written just a few months after the first letter, Paul's second epistle to the Thessalonians closely resembles the first. He undoubtedly wrote to clear up some misconceptions that his first letter may have left regarding the Lord's return. The first letter emphasizes what Christ's coming will mean for believers, both dead and alive. The second speaks more of the implications of the Lord's coming for "those who do not know God and do not obey the gospel of our Lord Jesus" (1:8). The second also includes a discussion of a rebellious "man of lawlessness" (2:1-10), who will display "every sort of evil that deceives those who are perishing" (2:10).

The Thessalonian Christians are suffering for their faith (1:5), and some of them think their tribulations are a sign of the end times. Not necessarily, Paul advises them. Their suffering will cease when Christ comes, for then it will be the turn of their persecutors to suffer. But before the day of the Lord a "rebellion" will reveal "the man of lawlessness," who will directly oppose and exalt himself over God.

What is important for the Thessalonians now is to "hold to the teachings we passed on to you" (2:15). Those who have been idle should go to work and support themselves (3:6-12). All the Christians should "never tire doing what is right" (3:13).

First and Second Thessalonians probably are Paul's earliest letters, with First and Second Corinthians following a few years later. These early epistles suggest that Paul preached frequently and enthusiastically about his Lord's coming. His writing on the theme is vivid. See 1 Corinthians 15:50-57 as well as 1 Thessalonians 4:16-18.

Paul's assurance of Christ's return was no less certain and no less eager in later years (Philippians 3:20, 21), but we do not read so much about it in the later epistles. Rather, Paul emphasizes the fact that Christ's decisive saving act has already been accomplished on the cross. What matters now is Christ's love expressed in His body, the church, and in every Christian's personal life. It is foolish to speculate about the time when Christ will come back. It is the better part of wisdom to so live that no matter when He comes, we will be ready—and this is emphasized in the early letters as well as the later ones. See 1 Corinthians 15:58; 2 Thessalonians 3:13. Like those early Christians, we must "never tire of doing what is right."

Test Your Knowledge

Mark each statement T for true or F for false.

_____ 1. The dominant theme of Philippians is concern about the second coming of Jesus.

_____ 2. Paul is discouraged because his friends in Philippi have been negligent of his needs in prison.

_____ 3. Judaizers are Jewish Christians who insist on obedience to the law of Moses as well as belief in Jesus Christ.

_____ 4. Paul seems to be torn between wanting to live and wanting to die.

_____ 5. Paul makes it clear that it is impossible for Christians really to imitate Jesus in any way.

_____ 6. The church at Thessalonica was one of the last congregations Paul founded before his imprisonment in Rome.

_____ 7. The Christians in Thessalonica were troubled about the second coming of Jesus.

_____ 8. Paul encourages all Christians to be very much concerned about the time of Jesus' return.

_____ 9. The second Thessalonian letter was written to correct a mistaken impression that some may have drawn from the first one.

_____ 10. Paul urges Christians to work for a living.

Letters on Organizing Churches

First and Second Timothy and Titus
1 Timothy 3:1-15; 2 Timothy 3:10-17

The two letters to Timothy and one to Titus are often called Pastoral Epistles. These three short letters share a common theme: How to be a church pastor. From a veteran church leader to his younger apprentices, they are filled with practical instructions concerning the proper way to *shepherd* the flock of Christ. (*Shepherd* is the literal meaning of *pastor*.)

From as early as the second century the authorship of these letters has been debated. The letters themselves plainly name Paul as the writer, but some scholars suspect another author used Paul's name to make his work more acceptable. "These letters contain too many words Paul never used in his other letters," the doubters declare. They add their belief that the letters indicate a developed church organization and a Gnostic heresy that belong to a time later than Paul's death. This belief makes them think these letters were written in that later time.

Those who believe Paul was the author are not disturbed by such doubts. They say the difference in vocabulary is accounted for by the difference in subject matter, and what we know about the church organization and the Gnostic heresy is not enough to prove that they did not exist in Paul's time. Most important of all, defenders of Paul's authorship point to the letters themselves. Each one claims to be the work of Paul. Those who accept this claim simply do not believe that any inspired book opens with a statement that is not true.

It seems that this evidence is not enough to convince the doubters, but it is too much to allow us to adopt their position. Even the doubters concede that the letters sound very much like the writing of Paul. If we accept them as really his, we find in them some hints of what he did in the later years of his life.

The book of Acts ends with the apostle a prisoner in Rome. It seems that he was released from prison, probably about A.D. 63, and went on with his traveling and teaching. He spent some time in the island of Crete, where he probably started a number of churches. There he left Titus to help the churches improve their organization and teaching (Titus 1:5). He visited Ephesus, where once he had taught for nearly three years. There he left Timothy to guide and help the church while Paul went on to Macedonia (1 Timothy 1:3). Probably he spent a winter in Nicopolis, in the western part of Greece (Titus 3:12). Earlier he had hoped to go to Spain (Romans 15:23, 24). Possibly he now fulfilled that wish. There is no hint of this in his letters, but near the end of the first century Clement of Rome writes of Paul's going to "the end of the west." At some point in his travels he wrote a letter to Timothy in Ephesus and another to Titus in Crete.

Perhaps about a year after Paul was set free to begin these travels, there was a disastrous fire in Rome. Some people suspected that the emperor himself had it started as a drastic kind of slum clearance. To divert suspicion from himself, Emperor Nero accused the Christians of setting Rome on fire. That was the excuse for a terrible persecution of the followers of Jesus.

Paul was an outstanding leader among Christians. In a few years he was again a prisoner (2 Timothy 1:8). This time he did not expect to be released for more travel on earth, but only for the waiting crown (2 Timothy 4:6-8). According to tradition, he was beheaded at Rome, and so went on to the "heavenly kingdom" (2 Timothy 4:18). But before he went he wrote his last epistle, the one we call 2 Timothy.

First Timothy 3:14, 15 states the theme of all three pastoral letters: "Although I hope to come to you soon, I am writing you these instructions so that, if I am delayed, you will know how people ought to conduct themselves in God's household." For this purpose Paul mixes practical and doctrinal matters, from instructions on selecting elders to warnings against Gnosticism.

It will be helpful for you to review the description of Gnosticism in chapter 8. Gnostics delight in the hidden meanings of words and tales and arguments. By their self-serving standard, only the intellectually elite can discover the secret truths that lead to salvation.

While some Gnostics favor unlimited self-indulgence, Paul calls for a disciplined life dedicated to God. He urges full participation in the good things of this world, including marriage and child-rearing, but he warns Timothy to flee from greed and to "pursue righteousness, godliness, faith, love, endurance, and gentleness" (1 Timothy 6:11). He repeatedly reminds his apprentices that our faith is in Christ. Sound doctrine teaches the preeminence of Christ; sound behavior exhibits love for brothers and sisters in Christ. As described in these letters, then, leadership of the church is concerned not so much with administrative efficiency as with protecting the faith. To this end Timothy and Titus should select and teach elders who exemplify Christian maturity untainted by heresy or questionable morality.

First Timothy

Immediately after his greeting Paul charges Timothy, the leader of the church at Ephesus, to prevent heretics from teaching their phony and dangerous doctrines (1:3-11). The Judaizers have one form of legalism and the Gnostics have another, but neither has a place in the church of Christ. Using himself as an example, Paul charges Timothy to hold fast to his faith in the merciful Christ and fight the *good* fight (1:12-20).

Chapter 2

Concerning public worship, Paul asks for prayers for everyone, especially those in authority. He affirms that there is only one mediator between God and man. (The Gnostics imagine a long series of emanations is necessary to bridge the gap between the goodness of God and the evil of man.) Men should pray with "holy hands": that is, hands dedicated to God and doing only good. Women may participate in prayers, but with modesty and propriety.

Chapter 3

For overseers and servants in the church (bishops and deacons) Paul sets a standard of personal character that avoids both the extremes of Gnosticism. The Gnostics suppose the human body is evil along with all other material things. Some Gnostics therefore punish this evil body by denying it any comfort or pleasure. Others take the opposite extreme. Thinking the body is incurably evil, they see no reason to restrain it. Anything it enjoys is permissible. But godliness is the standard Paul prescribes for elders (also called bishops) and deacons, who are models for the rest of the church. So are the deaconesses (or wives of the deacons—the Greek word could have either meaning) for women of the church. Every Christian should strive to live up to these standards that are set for elders and deacons.

Chapter 4
"Everything God created is good," Paul insists. No merit is gained by enforcing strict rules of diet or by denying oneself the pleasures of marriage. Timothy will teach his people this and encourage them to give thanks. He need not worry about his relative youth, because his example can be that of a mature man.

Chapter 5
Now for some advice about widows. Here Paul is very practical. Take care of widows who are in real need, but not those who live for pleasure. Older widows are to be cared for because they have served others. Younger ones should remarry, have children, and rear them well. A believing woman should care for her family's widows and not expect the church to do so.

Elders who do their job well are worthy of double honor. The word can also mean value or price. Since Paul adds, "The worker deserves his wages," some think he is saying the best elders should be paid so they can give their full time to the work. On the other hand, Timothy must rebuke even an elder if he proves unworthy. He must show no partiality.

And Timothy, says Paul, take care of your health!

Chapter 6
Slaves, respect your masters. Surely free employees should have no less regard for their employers. Otherwise they bring reproach on God and His church as well as themselves.

Beware of those who believe godliness is a way to get more money. Godliness itself, along with contentment, is worth more than money. "The love of money is a root of all kinds of evil."

Your task, Timothy, is to give yourself to such a positive Christian life that you will be found blameless when Jesus comes again. Command others also to put their hope in God, not in riches or speculation and debate. "Grace be with you."

Second Timothy

In what is generally considered the last of his letters, Paul writes from prison to his beloved son in the faith. This epistle repeats several of the concerns of the first letter, but concentrates more on Timothy's personal ministry. A significant feature is Paul's use of metaphors describing the ideal Christian minister (or the ideal Christian, for that matter). He is a

teacher (2:2),
  soldier (2:3),
    athlete (2:5),
      farmer (2:6),
        sufferer (2:8-13),
          workman (2:15),
            instrument (2:20, 21),
              servant (2:24).

A better known feature is Paul's tribute to the absolute authority and usefulness of the Scripture. It is God-breathed (inspired), so the preacher who uses it is "thoroughly equipped for every good work" (3:16, 17).

Chapters 1 and 2

From his greetings Paul moves quickly to encourage Timothy to remain faithful like his mother and grandmother, hanging on to his faith in spite of Paul's imprisonment. God is able to preserve us even though others may desert. Do not be a deserter, Timothy, but be a strong soldier or athlete. Remember Jesus, for whom I suffer, knowing that I shall be rewarded in Him (1:1—2:13).

Avoid becoming entangled in disputes and senseless controversies. Your task is to be a worthy workman, building on truth and not vain speculation. Youth may enjoy quarreling, but the mature servant of the Lord will be a kind and good teacher, hoping to teach even those who oppose Him (2:14-26).

Chapters 3 and 4

We face terrible times in which people give themselves over to godlessness. Do not worry, however: "They will not get very far because . . . their folly will be clear to everyone'' (3:1-9).

You know I have been persecuted, and so will all who want to live a godly life. You must continue in what you know from the Scriptures, because the Scriptures are inspired. You must preach them, having thoroughly prepared yourself, even in the face of opposition. I myself am ready to be sacrificed, for "I have fought the good fight . . . I have kept the faith," and I will be rewarded along with all of God's people (3:10—4:8).

After urging Timothy to come to him and relating some other personal notes, Paul closes with his final greetings (4:9-22).

Titus

Paul has left Titus on the island of Crete to finish organizing the churches which Paul himself probably established earlier. It seems that those congregations are small ones, living among people who have been described by one of their own poets as "liars, evil brutes, lazy gluttons" (1:12). A group of new Christians in such a culture is naturally having difficulty in attaining the standard of Christ.

Their difficulties are compounded by that heresy we have already met several times, Gnosticism. Add to that a touch of Jewish legalism, and you can see what Titus is up against.

Chapter 1

Titus must see that the very finest possible men are selected as elders—men who will be models for the rest. As in 1 Timothy 3, Paul calls for godly character and life. Since the church has many rebels, Titus must "rebuke them sharply" even as he holds up godly men to lead the church in truth.

Chapter 2

Titus must teach sound doctrine and upright personal behavior. He must demand that older men and women set an example for the younger, and that young men be self-controlled—and Titus also must be their example. He must teach the slaves trustworthiness, and teach everyone godliness. And he must teach with authority.

Chapter 3

Remind the people, Paul writes, to obey their authorities. Once we were all foolish and disobedient, but God saved us through baptism and the Holy Spirit given through Christ.

Avoid disputes about the law. Do not engage in unprofitable and useless controversies—and, after fair warning, avoid divisive persons.

Closing requests and greetings are in verses 12-15.

Test Your Knowledge

These letters give valuable advice for an organizing church. What does the author say about—

1. What to do with heretics in the church?

2. Who is the real mediator between God and man?

3. What is more important in church leaders, administrative skills or character traits?

4. What instructions has Paul for slaves?

5. How should a church take care of its widows?

6. Should church leaders be paid?

7. What is worth more than money?

8. What descriptive terms are used of a minister?

9. What makes the Scriptures reliable as a guide?

10. What does Paul say about obeying authorities?

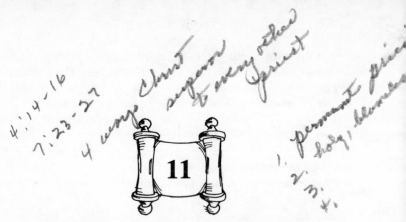

A Sermon to Jewish Christians

Hebrews
2:14-18; 4:14-16; 7:23-28; 12:1-13

Hebrews is listed among the epistles, and indeed it closes like a personal letter. Most of the book, however, reads like a sermon or series of sermons. In the style of first-century preaching, Hebrews is based largely on Psalms 2, 8, 95, and 110 and Jeremiah 31:31-34. Passages are cited and then interpreted in light of revelation in Christ. Finally the preacher makes practical applications and challenges his listeners to put them into practice. This book is rightly called a "word of exhortation": that is, a sermon for Christians rather than an evangelistic appeal to non-Christians (13:22).

We don't know who wrote Hebrews. Debate about its authorship has raged from ancient times, with some naming Paul, others Apollos, still others Barnabas or someone else. Hebrews differs in many ways from Paul's letters, yet there is no evidence to show that it is the work of any other person. Hebrews is usually attributed simply to "the writer."

The question of date is equally unanswerable, with scholars divided between an earlier date between A.D. 60 and 70 and a later time around A.D. 85.

What does not seem debatable, however, is that the writer is a Jew who is equally at home with Old Testament literature and Greek culture.

10:19-25
12:1-2

We do not know to whom Hebrews was originally sent. A fair guess is that it went to persecuted Jewish Christians in Rome. There were persecuted Jewish Christians in many places, however. Some students suppose the letter was sent to Jerusalem.

To Jewish Christians in some place, the writer sent this well-reasoned exhortation as a reminder of their hope in Christ and an encouragement to remain steadfast even in suffering. Apparently they were being verbally abused, and some were losing property just because they believed in Jesus. But as the author reminds them, they have not yet joined Christ in shedding their blood for His cause (12:3, 4). Bloodshed may come, however, so he urges them repeatedly to endure their trials with patience.

He strengthens his readers by convincing them of the absolute superiority of Jesus Christ. Union with Him is worth any hardship. The argument of the epistle rests on three major propositions:

The person of Christ is superior (1:1—4:13).
The priesthood of Christ is superior (4:14—10:18).
Your life in Christ is superior to any other you can choose (10:19—13:21).

The Superiority of Christ's Person

The writer immediately establishes Jesus' preeminence over Old Testament prophets. He is God's Son, heir of all things, Creator of the universe, the radiance of God's glory, the exact image of His being, sustainer of everything, redeemer and ruler (1:1-3). He surpasses not only prophets but also angels, as several Scriptures prove (1:4-14). It is imperative, then, to listen to Him and not defect from His teaching (2:1-4).

Angels, after all, do not rule the world; but Jesus does. He was perfected through suffering. We belong to His family, because He became like us to free us and become our high priest. He made it possible for us to be united again with God (2:5-18).

God has made Jesus greater than Moses, the lawgiver, just as the builder is greater than the house he builds. Or, to change the figure slightly, God builds the house and Moses serves in the house (Israel), but Jesus is the Son who is over every servant. We must be loyal to Jesus then, preventing one another from rebelling as the followers of Moses did (3:1-19).

The Israelite rebels failed to receive rest in the promised land because they grumbled and disobeyed. We dare not follow their

91

example, or we shall lose the eternal rest from work and suffering that God has promised us. He sees everything, and His Word penetrates our innermost being. We can't fool Him, so we had better obey Him (4:1-13).

The Superiority of Christ's Priesthood

Christ is superior to every other priest because:

1. Other high priests are mortal. They serve for a time and are replaced. Christ died and was raised. He has no successors; He is priest forever (7:23, 24).

2. Other priests have to offer sacrifices over and over. Christ offered His once for all (7:27).

3. Other priests are sinners who need forgiveness along with their people. Christ was and is sinless (4:15—5:3).

4. Christ is of the superior priesthood ("the order of Melchizedek") promised in Scriptures (4:14—5:10; Genesis 14:17-20).

Since these things are true, you must pass beyond a diet of elementary teachings and go on to the meat of mature thinking about Christ. Remain steadfast, for if you fall away you will be beyond repentance. Produce a useful crop by your diligence in faith and work (5:11—6:12).

You can place your confidence in God, because He keeps His promises. He did so with Abraham and He does so through our eternal high priest, Jesus. Jesus is like Melchizedek, to whom Abraham gave a tithe of everything in recognition of his greatness. Perfection was not attained through the Levitical priesthood, but has now been achieved in the person of Jesus, "a priest forever, in the order of Melchizedek."With a new priest has come a new law, or more accurately, a new covenant between God and His people (6:13—7:28).

It is not just a *new* but a *better* covenant. Our high priest offers gifts and sacrifices in Heaven. He is the superior high priest of the superior covenant foretold in Jeremiah 31:31-34.

The first covenant governed regulations for worship in the holy tent (tabernacle), so that when the high priest entered the Most Holy Place once a year he could make the sin offering. But this act could not give people a clear conscience. It took the blood of Christ, who "went through the greater and more perfect tabernacle that is not man-made," doing so with the offering of His blood. He has cleansed our consciences and we can now serve the living God.

He has become the mediator of a new covenant. Moses consecrated the earlier agreement with blood sprinkled on the scroll, the people, the tabernacle, and the instruments of worship. Christ entered Heaven itself, however, not having to offer sacrifices of blood every year, because He offered His own blood once and for all. His next appearance will not be to bear sin—He has already done that—but to save those who wait for Him.

Let there be no misunderstanding. Christ has ended the ritual of annual sin offerings by the high priest through His once-for-all offering of His own blood. Now our high priest rules at the right hand of God, having done what was necessary to perfect those who are in Him. They are forgiven; no additional sacrifice for sin is needed (8:1—10:18).

The Superiority of Life in Christ

With all this in mind, we know that we can come into God's presence with confidence. We are cleansed with Christ's blood and baptized in pure water in His name. Since He is faithful, let us be faithful also. Encourage one another to love and good deeds. Meet together faithfully as you await His second coming. To deliberately keep on sinning is to forfeit all that He has promised and "fall into the hands of the living God." You used to be strong in suffering. Be so now (10:19-39).

Imitate the examples of the great heroes of faith. They were sure of what they hoped for and certain of what they could not see, these heroes like Abel, Enoch, Noah, Abraham, and many others. They "were all commended for their faith" (11:1-40).

With these witnesses all around us, let us be equally persevering as we follow Jesus through opposition. You haven't yet suffered as He did; endure your hardships as sons whom a father loves and disciplines for their good (12:1-13).

Live peacefully with everybody and be upright. You are citizens of Heavenly Jerusalem, God's own city, living in the presence of God and His angels and Jesus who brought you a new covenant. Heed God's warning, and be thankful. Worship God with reverence and awe.

Pay attention to these several warnings and exhortations, continually giving God praise and sharing with one another. Obey your leaders—they are there to protect you. Pray for us, too. May God "equip you with everything good for doing His will" (12:14—13:25).

Test Your Knowledge

1. Hebrews makes three major statements:

   The _~~person priesthood~~_ love of Christ is superior.

   The _person_ of Christ is superior.

   Your _life_ in Christ is superior.

2. Christ is superior to both prophets and _angels_.

3. Jesus is greater than Moses the lawgiver just as the _____ _builder_ of a house is greater than the house itself.

4. The order of Melchizedek is a superior order of _priests_.

5. You can place your confidence in God, because He keeps His _promises_.

6. The covenant Christ brings is not only new but _better_ than the old one.

7. Through His blood Christ has cleansed our _sins_.

8. We can now come into God's presence with _confidence_.

9. The heroes listed in chapter 11 "were all commended for their _faith_."

10. You are citizens of _heavenly_ Jerusalem.

Letters of Instruction
For Christian Living

James, 1 and 2 Peter, Jude
James 2:14-26; 1 Peter 1:13-24; 2 Peter 3:11-18

With the passing of decades, correspondence from Christian leaders to young churches and immature Christians became increasingly important. As the churches grew, so did the opposition that came from governmental and Jewish sources and also from within the congregations themselves. Heresies and unseemly personal conduct had to be corrected. Hence these letters.

James

The theme of this letter, traditionally attributed to James the brother of Jesus, is that faith in Christ is to be put to work in practical activities like looking after orphans and widows and keeping oneself from being polluted by the world (1:27).

As is fitting from a leader of the Jerusalem church, James' letter is thoroughly Jewish in its ethical applications of the faith. He praises believers who don't desert under pressure and rebukes those who do. Steeped in wisdom literature of the Old Testament, James pens sentences that often sound like New Testament proverbs and wise sayings.

He warns the rich, the self-indulgent, the argumentative, the talkative, the proud and complaining and deceitful to practice what they say they believe. Martin Luther centuries later was offended because James would not agree that one is saved by faith *alone* (Paul would not have said so either, by the way), but that faith is proved by deeds.

Some scholars have guessed an early date (A.D. 45) for the letter; others think it must have been written around A.D. 60 or later, when Christians of the second and third generation were tending to lose something of the personal relationship with God and were defining faith more as a set of beliefs. Perhaps some thought they were "faithful" if they just mouthed proper statements of belief. James destroys that idea. He says faith not substantiated by works is dead.

Paul emphasized faith in Christ to correct the Jews who relied on works of the law as the road to salvation. James emphasized works to correct the false impression that mere acceptance of true doctrines will assure salvation. We need both Paul and James.

James' teaching often parallels that of Jesus, as you can see by comparing the following verses from this letter with Jesus' Sermon on the Mount:

James	Matthew
2:14-26	7:21-23
1:22	7:24-27
3:11, 12	7:16-20
4:11, 12	7:1
5:1-6	6:19-24
5:12	5:34-37

As you read through James' letter, look especially for:
1. Encouragement in trying times (1:2-18).
2. The importance of doing as well as listening (1:19-27).
3. Chastisement for showing partiality (2:1-13).
4. The relationship of faith to work (2:14-26).
5. The necessity of bridling your tongue (3:1-12).
6. A definition of true wisdom (3:13-18).
7. Submission to God to avoid contention (4:1-17).
8. The peril of riches (5:1-6).
9. The rewards of patience and prayer (5:7-20).

First Peter

Scholars heatedly debate almost everything about the writing of this letter. Some insist it is by Peter, others just as insistently say it cannot be. Some flatly state that it was written to Christian Gentiles in Asia Minor; others say it was written to Christian Jews. It was written in the sixties according to some; it was very late, end of the century, say others. However, there seems to be no compelling reason to doubt the books's own statement that Simon Peter wrote it to Christians scattered in Asia Minor. Probably the time was the middle sixties of the first century.

What no one argues about is its timeless relevance to Christian believers everywhere. *Suffering* is the key word, which the author discusses with unwavering hopefulness. Whether Christians face ridicule or accusations of treachery against the government or whatever, they can be certain of victory if they trust their souls to God with humility. In this respect, 1 Peter resembles two other letters of encouragement, Romans and Hebrews.

Suffering can be accepted with joy because Christians are God's people, redeemed and purified and reborn, forgiven and saved. Consider the following expressions:

1:3. "In his great mercy he has given us new birth into a living hope."

1:18. "For you know . . . you were redeemed from the empty way of life handed down to you from your forefathers."

1:22. "You have purified yourselves by obeying the truth."

1:23. "For you have been born again."

2:2. "Like newborn babes, crave pure spiritual milk, so that by it you may grow up in your salvation."

2:10. "Now you have received mercy."

3:21. "This water symbolizes baptism that now saves you . . . by the resurrection of Jesus Christ."

With praise to God for bringing about in Christ the salvation for which prophets long have hoped, Peter calls his readers to live holy lives of mutual love and of trust in the imperishable Word of God (chapter 1).

Christians are to act as God's very own people in the world, offering themselves in His service, proclaiming His praises so that others may be saved. To that end Christians must separate themselves from sin and its consequences. This includes submitting to earthly authorities, as Christ himself did (chapter 2).

Similarly, wives should submit to husbands and husbands should be considerate of wives. All Christians should live together in harmony. Yes, you will suffer—but it is far better to suffer for good than for evil. Christ himself died for doing good,

97

and we who are united with Him in baptism are like Noah and his family, who were saved through the water. The water alone does not save us, of course, but the resurrection of Jesus Christ does (chapter 3).

Prepare to suffer as Christ did, living for God and not for physical pleasure. Because the end is near, you must live for God with the strength He provides. Rejoice that you can share His suffering, and continue to do good (chapter 4).

To this end, elders, take care of your people. Be good shepherds of God's flock. You young men, honor your elders. All of you, be self-controlled and alert to the threat of the devil. God will take care of you (chapter 5).

Second Peter

Second Peter has long been the object of debate among Bible scholars. As early as the second century, questions were raised about who wrote this excellent letter, or when, or to whom. For the purposes of this study, however, we'll accept Peter's authorship and move quickly on to the message, which resonates with apostolic truth.

That apostolic truth calls wavering Christians to hold fast to God's truth in Christ. First Peter deals with persecution. Second Peter speaks of false teaching, especially that enemy we have become quite familiar with by now, Gnosticism. You remember that Gnostics ("know-it-alls") believed that spirit is good and matter is evil. Some of them used that belief to justify grossly immoral behavior, saying that what the body does cannot affect the spirit. Here is Peter's response.

You can escape the corruption of evil desires because God has given you everything needed for godliness. Hang on to your knowledge of Christ, which is not from somebody's fertile imagination but is historical fact. I know, for I was an eyewitness of His transfiguration. Further, the prophecies of old, inspired by the Holy Spirit, have been fulfilled in Him (chapter 1).

But you must beware of false teachers who deny the Lord, who make up stories, and who will be condemned by the God who spared neither angels nor men nor cities when they sinned. These blasphemers now trying to deceive you will be paid back for the harm they have done. Their destiny is terrible (chapter 2).

Scoffers raise questions like, "When is Christ coming?" They imply that He is not coming. But as waters once flooded the world and destroyed it, so the fire will one day destroy it as God has promised. Judgment is coming, but only God, with whom "a day is like a thousand years, and a thousand years are like a day," knows exactly when. But be certain it is coming.

What is important, then, is the kind of people you must be: holy and godly as you eagerly await the destruction of this heaven and earth but the coming of a new one for the righteous. In the meantime, patiently and blamelessly wait (chapter 3).

Jude

Jude appears here because it closely resembles 2 Peter. Honored tradition has it that the author of this letter was a brother of the James who wrote the book of James, and therefore another of Jesus' half brothers (Matthew 13:55). The name *Jude* is the same as *Judas,* but we use the short form to distinguish this good Christian from the well-known traitor. It may have been between A.D. 70 and 80 when Jude wrote his letter. Some students think it was more probably between 60 and 70.

Like Peter, Jude warns his readers against members whose unChristian character is a threat to the church. Jude does not spare his vocabulary as he describes them. They are "godless," "dreamers," "unreasoning animals," "blemishes," "shepherds who feed only themselves," "clouds without rain," "autumn trees, without fruit and uprooted," "wild waves of the sea," "wandering stars," "grumblers and faultfinders," and "scoffers."

With these slippery characters in their ranks, true Christians must contend for the faith, remembering how God has always dealt with such persons and how the apostles warned they would adulterate the pure church. You Christians, therefore, must be strong in the faith, keeping yourselves in God's love, and trusting Him "who is able to keep you from falling."

Test Your Knowledge

1. The theme of James is (a) steadfastness in suffering, (b) faith expressed in deeds, (c) joy in sorrow.

2. The book of James was written by (a) James the apostle, (b) James the half brother of Jesus, (c) some person now unknown.

3. Which of these ideas does James *not* discuss: (a) the role of Christ as our high priest, (b) the rewards of patience and prayer, (c) the necessity of bridling your tongue.

4. The key word of 1 Peter is (a) sanctification, (b) grace, (c) suffering.

5. First Peter is addressed to (a) the church in Rome, (b) scattered Christians in Asia Minor, (c) Jews in Jerusalem.

6. First Peter describes Christians as people (a) redeemed and reborn, (b) defeated and hopeless, (c) not subject to worldly rulers.

7. Peter assures Christians (a) they need to be alert to the threat of the devil, (b) they have nothing to fear from the devil, (c) they can do nothing to protect themselves from the devil.

8. Second Peter deals with the threat of (a) Judaism, (b) Gnosticism, (c) Phariseeism.

9. Second Peter says God has given us everything needed for (a) prosperity, (b) success, (c) godliness.

10. Jude's warning is against (a) outsiders who would hurt the church, (b) members whose un-Christian character threatens the church, (c) government officials who persecute the church.

The Letters and Revelation of John

1 John 4:7-21; Revelation 21:1-8

The Gospel, three letters, and Revelation of John have been traditionally bundled together as the "Johannine Literature." We have already looked at the Gospel. Now we turn to these brief letters and that long and strange document, Revelation, that stands at the end of our Bible.

First John

According to early church tradition, the apostle John made his home in Ephesus after Jerusalem was destroyed in A.D. 70. In his old age he wrote the message we call 1 John. It is addressed to people well known and very dear to him. He calls them not only "brethren," but also "beloved" and "my little children." (See 1 John 2:1, 7; 3:2 in the King James Version. The New International Version departs from literal translation in favor of more modern terms in these verses.) These dear friends probably were Christians John had taught in Ephesus and other cities of the area. Some students suggest that John may have written the letter when he could not teach in person because he was a prisoner on Patmos (Revelation 1:9).

In vocabulary and writing style, 1 John and the Gospel of John are so similar that we can hardly doubt they are the work of the same man. Some later scholars, however, have concluded that

101

the writer was not John the apostle, but another leader of the same name, probably in Ephesus. Such questions about the human author need not disturb us if we realize that the writing is inspired, a timeless message from God.

Timeless is the right word. Like John's Gospel, 1 John abounds in large, eternal thoughts. John speaks frequently of the Father, the Son, the Spirit, the beginning, and the Word. He stresses belief, life, light, love, and abiding. He speaks of keeping eternal commandments in the comfort of the Spirit. The letters offer the distilled wisdom of a very old man who is guided by the Holy Spirit. He has no energy to waste on trivia. He knows what is important and gives himself to that.

He knows. This epistle of assurance uses *"we know"* thirteen times and related words of knowing at least forty times. You can't fool John; he has lived too long, seen too much, overcome too often to be led away from the truth. Besides, he is inspired by the Holy Spirit. His hope is to save his readers from the pitfalls of spiritual detours. He wants them to know what he knows and enjoy the security he has found in the Lord.

Writing to believers whose spiritual condition is not robust, he warns of the disastrous consequences of sin and worldliness, especially the sin of indifference to a brother's physical needs (1 John 3:17, 18). Christians must love one another, because love is of God (1 John 4:7). They may well doubt their personal salvation if they are not believing with love and experiencing the joy of their salvation.

Now let's try to summarize the main thoughts of 1 John.

The word of life (1:1-4). John is combatting that familiar enemy, Gnosticism. In this prologue he stresses the physical reality of Christ's body. Gnostics may say that Christ only *seemed* to be present in a physical body, but they can't tell John that. He has seen for himself—even touched that real physical body.

The opposition of sin and belief (1:5–2:6). We cannot walk down two paths; either we follow God to light or pursue sin to eternal darkness. We can't pretend to be sinless, but we can confess sin and triumph over it through Jesus Christ. We follow God and avoid sin through obeying Christ.

Belief expressed in love (2:7-11). Christian faith without love is not possible. If anyone claims to believe in Christ but does not love, he is in darkness.

A call to flee the world (2:12-17). This is a call not to put one's trust in the world's values. Young and old must choose the eternal will of God and not the fickle pleasures of the world.

A call to flee false teachers (2:18-29). Jesus has His enemies, even in church. The Spirit of truth will protect you from the antichrist who denies Father and Son. Remain in the Spirit.

A call to moral purity (3:1-10). Like true children of God, live without sinning.

Love one another (3:11-24). This is the true test of your love for God. Love as Jesus loved, to the death. Don't just talk of love—show it!

A test for truth (4:1-6). The test of a spirit is sincere willingness to acknowledge the truth of Christ's human existence. Whoever is of God will listen to others who are from Him.

Another test (4:7-21). True believers love one another. Love is the test, as is life in the Spirit who enables us to confess Jesus as Son of God. Those who really love God in Christ will love one another.

The results of faith in Christ (5:1-12). We will carry out His commands in love, thus overcoming the world. Since the Spirit, the water, and the blood testify of Jesus' divinity, we believe in Him; and in Him we have life.

A final word of assurance (5:13-21). John has written so that we may *know* we have eternal life. If we are God's, we will not continue in sin. Through Christ, we know the truth and are in Him.

Second John

This brief note warns a Christian woman of the perils of thoughtless comradery with "deceivers who do not acknowledge Jesus Christ as coming in the flesh." The author is again attacking Gnosticism, which in one of its forms denies that God appeared on earth in human flesh. Gnosticism is no minor departure from Christian doctrine; it attacks the very basis of Christian faith.

We must love one another with the understanding that love holds fast to loved ones and necessarily separates the obedient to the Father from the disobedient.

Third John

This personal letter praises Gaius, an active, generous layman whose hospitality on behalf of his church—especially by hosting visiting preachers—significantly assists the Christian cause. Unfortunately, Gaius' church is in trouble because Diotrephes, with unconverted ego, promotes himself instead of submitting to the authority of the church's real leaders. His example is to be rejected as surely as that of Gaius and Demetrius is to be imitated.

Revelation

What shall we make of this peculiar book, Revelation? It seems to defy our understanding even as it threatens us if we add or take away anything (22:18, 19). How can a book about candlesticks and many-headed monsters and singing angels be of any use to a twentieth-century Christian? How seriously should we take a book that has confused millions of readers through the centuries and certainly has been misinterpreted by many?

We obviously can't do it justice in a few brief pages, nor can we present even a few of the wildly conflicting theories forced on the book, let alone reconcile them. So what follows is just one man's opinion.

Revelation may not be entirely clear to modern readers, but its theme cannot be missed: Jesus will win. Written to persecuted first-century Christians, Revelation insists that things are not what they seem. The church appears to be in trouble and Satan appears to be winning. Not so, John proclaims. Enemies may make war against the Lamb (Christ), but Jesus will conquer and His followers will be with Him (17:14). Let the beasts roar and the soldiers of Satan attack. They cannot win. Christ is conqueror (1:18; 2:8; 5:9-13; 6:2; 11:15; 12:9, 10; 14:1, 14; 15:2-4; 19:16; 22:3-5).

First-century Christians needed Revelation. When the Roman emperor decreed that everyone in his empire, including Christians, must worship him, Christians faced death. What should they do? Resist him, John tells them, and resist his lord, Satan. You may seem to be losing, but God has already decreed that His Son will reign forever with those who belong to Him, and Satan will be conquered forever.

John's message from the Lord becomes quite specific in the letters to churches in Asia Minor (chapters 2 and 3). There are seven of them (a number representing completeness, these seven representing the whole Christian community) and they are troubled. Pergamum worshiped the emperor long before his worship became Rome's official religion; hence the reference to Satan's throne. Sardis had once been captured as by a thief when her seemingly impregnable acropolis was entered through a tiny crevice, to the surprise and defeat of the fabled King Croesus. The church in Sardis must be more alert than Croesus, or the Lord will come and destroy it. Laodicea, site of a famous hospital dedicated to Aesculapius, god of healing, holds a church that is blinded by wealth, unable to see its own nakedness. What the Spirit writes to the seven churches must be heeded by all churches of all time.

Although unique among New Testament books, Revelation is similar to many other books produced between 200 B.C. and A.D. 100. These works are called apocalyptic, which means disclosing, uncovering. They were born in a time of trouble. As the writers see it, the world is in terrible shape and man cannot cope. He will be overcome by its evil unless God intervenes. But God will intervene, the writers promise. This day's evil will give way under God's power to a glorious new day, the Day of the Lord.

Some of the apocalypses were wishful thinking bolstered with Old Testament prophecies. Some of the later books probably were influenced also by promises of Jesus. Revelation towers above them all because it is a genuine revelation from God. Christians quickly recognized it as God's word about their coming triumph in Christ.

Revelation promises a divine Messiah who will overthrow Satan. There will be a time of terror, the world will be profoundly shaken, human relationships broken, judgment meted out, the dead raised, and a new Jerusalem established to replace the disgraced earthly habitation of God's people. In that holy city all enmity will cease and harmony will prevail among men and between man and his new world. There will be no more tears—the Lord will reign.

Remember, Revelation was for first-century Christians. Its first readers must have seen that it was written to assure *them* of God's comfort and Jesus' victory. Revelation is God's answer to their prayers and tears in time of trouble. As they read its pages they could identify their enemies in the dragon (12:3), the beast (13:1), the false prophet (16:13), and Babylon (14:8). They could celebrate the downfall of those enemies (18:2; 19:20; 20:10). God was speaking directly to them:

I see your tears and will end them (7:17; 21:4)

Be faithful and you will win (2:10).

105

Your Lord lives and reigns forever (11:15).

Rather than search the book for a history lesson or a step-by-step guide to the future, we shall read it as a promise, repeated with different symbols, of Christ's victory and Satan's defeat. We shall see that it speaks to us as clearly and powerfully as to Christians of the first century. We shall see that it reveals events beyond the time of those early Christians (1:19; 4:1) and beyond our present time (chapters 21, 22).

It is helpful to read Revelation with Genesis. In the Bible's first book we learn of man's rebellion against God and his subsequent curse. Death is introduced in Genesis, but Revelation contains the conquest of death, the removal of sin and its consequences, and a new heaven and earth to replace those of Genesis.

Looking for the grand themes in Revelation convinces us that, whatever the historical allusions, Revelation pictures typical events. Some of its prophecies may be fulfilled again and again.

Everyone who reads or hears the words of this prophecy can indeed be blessed (1:3), no matter what his century. The truth presented is timeless.

Here is a brief synopsis of the action.

I. Prologue (chapter 1).

John introduces his visions and identifies their source as Jesus. Note Jesus' physical appearance (1:12-16) and His authority based on His resurrection (1:18).

II. Letters to the Seven Churches (chapters 2 and 3)

Ephesus (2:1-7), a hard-working church that has forsaken her first love.

Smyrna (2:8-11), a church poor in money but rich in faith.

Pergamum (2:12-17), the church "where Satan has his throne," faithful but imperfect.

Thyatira (2:18-28), troubled by immorality.

Sardis (3:1-6), reputed to be alive, but really dead.

Philadelphia (3:7-13), with an open door that no one can shut.

Laodicea (3:14-22), lukewarm and indifferent.

III. Worship of God and the Lamb (4:1—5:14)

Surrounded by twenty-four elders (representing all the people of God, Old and New Covenants) and four living

106

creatures, God receives honor and glory. His Son is proclaimed worthy to open the scroll and reveal the future through the seals. Praise of the Son arises from every creature in Heaven and earth and sea.

IV. **The Seven Seals (6:1—8:1)**
The first four seals: the four horsemen (6:1-8).
The fifth seal: cry of the martyrs (6:9-11).
The sixth seal: a great earthquake (6:12-17).
Interlude: sealing of 144,000 from Israel; praise of a great multitude from all nations (7:1-17).
The seventh seal: heavenly silence (8:1).

V. **The Seven Trumpets (8:2—11:19).**
The offering of incense (8:2-5).
The first four trumpets and the eagles's warning (8:6-13).
The fifth trumpet: locusts of torment (9:1-12).
The sixth trumpet: cavalry of death (9:13-21).
Interlude: two visions.
   The mighty angel and the little scroll (10:1-11).
   The two witnesses (11:1-14).
The seventh trumpet: praise the Lord (11:15-19).

VI. **Conflict Between the Church and Satan (12:1—14:20).**
The woman, dragon, and man child (12:1-6).
War in heaven (12:7-12).
War on earth (12:13-17).
Beasts from sea and earth (13:1-18).
The new song (14:1-5).
Pictures of the final judgment (14:6-20).

VII. **The Seven Last Plagues (15:1—16:21).**
The seven angels with seven plagues (15:1-8).
The seven bowls of God's wrath (16:1-21).

VIII. **The Downfall of Babylon (17:1—19:5).**
The woman on the beast (17:1-18).
The destruction of Babylon proclaimed (18:1-8).
Babylon lamented (18:9-20).
Babylon dead (18:21-24).
Heaven rejoicing (19:1-5).

IX. God's Final Victory (19:6—20:15)
The marriage of the lamb announced (19:6-10).
The Messiah on a white horse (19:11-16).
End of beast and false prophet (19:17-21).
Doom of Satan (20:1-10).
Judgment of the dead (20:11-15).

X. New Heaven and New Earth (21:1—22:5)

XI. John's Final Words (22:6-21)

Test Your Knowledge

True—False

1. __T__ Johannine literature includes the Gospel of John, three letters of John, and Revelation.
2. __T__ Ancient tradition indicates that John lived in Ephesus in his old age.
3. __T__ John could tell accurately about Jesus because he knew Jesus personally.
4. __F__ The letters of John deal with specific, practical problems in the churches.
5. __F__ John admits that those who really love God often do not love each other.
6. __T__ Second John is an attack on the false teachings of Gnosticism.
7. __F__ Revelation is literature of a type that was popular in the first century, but it has nothing much to say to our day.
8. __F__ Revelation is encouraging to us, but it didn't mean much to the first readers because the final victory was centuries away.
9. __F__ The major theme of Revelation is the awesome power of Satan. *That Christ will win.*
10. __T__ It is good to read Revelation with Genesis, because it presents a new heaven and earth to replace those spoiled by man's sin recorded in Genesis.

Other Books by
LeRoy Lawson

The Lord of Promises
A Book about the Lord who promises and keeps His promises.

The Lord of Possibilities
A study of Christ's miracles.

Cracking the Code
Unlocks some of the more useful secrets of the kingdom of heaven from Jesus' parables.

Up From Chaos: Genesis Today
Lawson concentrates not on solving the problem raised by Genesis, but on demonstrating the book's relevance for today.

Books are available from Standard Publishing
or from your local supplier.